W9-BZM-841

Writing the Critical Essay

Teen Pregnancy

An OPPOSING  VIEWPOINTS® Guide

Lauri S. Friedman, *Book Editor*

**OPPOSING
VIEWPOINTS®
SERIES**

GREENHAVEN PRESS
A part of Gale, Cengage Learning

GALE
CENGAGE Learning™

Detroit • New York • San Francisco • New Haven, Conn • Waterville, Maine • London

Christine Nasso, *Publisher*
Elizabeth Des Chenes, *Managing Editor*

© 2010 Greenhaven Press, a part of Gale, Cengage Learning

Gale and Greenhaven Press are registered trademarks used herein under license.

For more information, contact:
Greenhaven Press
27500 Drake Rd.
Farmington Hills, MI 48331-3535
Or you can visit our Internet site at gale.cengage.com

For product information and technology assistance, contact us at

Gale Customer Support, 1-800-877-4253
For permission to use material from this text or product, submit all requests online at www.cengage.com/permissions

Further permissions questions can be e-mailed to permissionrequest@cengage.com

Articles in Greenhaven Press anthologies are often edited for length to meet page requirements. In addition, original titles of these works are changed to clearly present the main thesis and to explicitly indicate the author's opinion. Every effort is made to ensure that Greenhaven Press accurately reflects the original intent of the authors. Every effort has been made to trace the owners of copyrighted material.

Cover image © 2010 Photos.com, a division of Getty Images. All rights reserved.

LIBRARY OF CONGRESS CATALOGING-IN-PUBLICATION DATA

Teen pregnancy / Lauri S. Friedman, book editor.
    p. cm. -- (Writing the critical essay: an opposing viewpoints guide)
  Includes bibliographical references and index.
  ISBN 978-0-7377-4804-8 (hardcover)
  1. Teenage pregnancy--Juvenile literature. 2. Sex instruction for teenagers--Juvenile literature. 3. Emergency contraceptives--Juvenile literature. I. Friedman, Lauri S.
  HQ759.4.T4219 2010
  613.9'55--dc22
                                                          2010000919

Printed in the United States of America
1 2 3 4 5 6 7 14 13 12 11 10

CONTENTS

Examining the state of writing and how it is taught in the United States was the official purpose of the National Commission on Writing in America's Schools and Colleges. The commission, made up of teachers, school administrators, business leaders, and college and university presidents, released its first report in 2003. "Despite the best efforts of many educators," commissioners argued, "writing has not received the full attention it deserves." Among the findings of the commission was that most fourth-grade students spent less than three hours a week writing, that three-quarters of high school seniors never receive a writing assignment in their history or social studies classes, and that more than 50 percent of first-year students in college have problems writing error-free papers. The commission called for a "cultural sea change" that would increase the emphasis on writing for both elementary and secondary schools. These conclusions have made some educators realize that writing must be emphasized in the curriculum. As colleges are demanding an ever-higher level of writing proficiency from incoming students, schools must respond by making students more competent writers. In response to these concerns, the SAT, an influential standardized test used for college admissions, required an essay for the first time in 2005.

Books in the Writing the Critical Essay: An Opposing Viewpoints Guide series use the patented Opposing Viewpoints format to help students learn to organize ideas and arguments and to write essays using common critical writing techniques. Each book in the series focuses on a particular type of essay writing—including expository, persuasive, descriptive, and narrative—that students learn while being taught both the five-paragraph essay as well as longer pieces of writing that have an opinionated focus. These guides include everything necessary to help students research, outline, draft, edit, and ultimately write successful essays across the curriculum, including essays for the SAT.

Using Opposing Viewpoints

This series is inspired by and builds upon Greenhaven Press's acclaimed Opposing Viewpoints series. As in the parent series, each book in the Writing the Critical Essay series focuses on a timely and controversial social issue that provides lots of opportunities for creating thought-provoking essays. The first section of each volume begins with a brief introductory essay that provides context for the opposing viewpoints that follow. These articles are chosen for their accessibility and clearly stated views. The thesis of each article is made explicit in the article's title and is accentuated by its pairing with an opposing or alternative view. These essays are both models of persuasive writing techniques and valuable research material that students can mine to write their own informed essays. Guided reading and discussion questions help lead students to key ideas and writing techniques presented in the selections.

The second section of each book begins with a preface discussing the format of the essays and examining characteristics of the featured essay type. Model five-paragraph and longer essays then demonstrate that essay type. The essays are annotated so that key writing elements and techniques are pointed out to the student. Sequential, step-by-step exercises help students construct and refine thesis statements; organize material into outlines; analyze and try out writing techniques; write transitions, introductions, and conclusions; and incorporate quotations and other researched material. Ultimately, students construct their own compositions using the designated essay type.

The third section of each volume provides additional research material and writing prompts to help the student. Additional facts about the topic of the book serve as a convenient source of supporting material for essays. Other features help students go beyond the book for their research. Like other Greenhaven Press books, each book in the Writing the Critical Essay series includes bibliographic listings of relevant periodical articles, books, Web sites, and organizations to contact.

Writing the Critical Essay: An Opposing Viewpoints Guide will help students master essay techniques that can be used in any discipline.

Teen Pregnancy and Adoption

Pregnant teens find themselves with few options for dealing with their situation, and none are ideal. According to the Gladney Center for Adoption and the organization Child Trends, the majority of pregnant teens—about 51 percent—choose to give birth and keep their baby. Yet those who raise a child as a teenager are more likely to live in poverty, never get married, and not finish high school or college and have a career. These realities make having a baby as a teenager a difficult and consequence-ridden choice. Yet for the 35 percent of teens who choose to terminate their pregnancies, life is not much simpler. Some report feeling regret over their decision to abort their baby, and those who are encouraged by their parents to get an abortion against their will are more than twice as likely to end up pregnant again within a year. Another 14 percent of pregnant teens miscarry early enough in their pregnancy to avoid being faced with the decision. Finally, there are teens who choose to give birth and place the baby for adoption. This is a difficult and controversial decision, and fewer than 1 percent of pregnant teens choose it.

Adoption rates were not always so low. In the 1940s and 1950s, before abortion was legal in the United States, Planned Parenthood estimates that 95 percent of unmarried teenage mothers placed their child for adoption. But after *Roe v. Wade* legalized abortion in 1973, many fewer teens chose this emotionally wrought route. Today, according to the National Committee for Adoption and the group Physicians for Reproductive Choice and Health, only 2 to 3 percent of pregnant teens make a plan to give the baby up for adoption. After they give birth, not all of them go through with the idea, and thus fewer than 1 percent of babies born to unmarried teenagers actually end up being placed with adoptive parents.

In a rare offering, the 2007 movie *Juno* tackled the issues of teen pregnancy and adoption in a unique and memorable way, though the movie sparked much debate over the message it sent to pregnant teens about the difficulties and realties of placing an unwanted baby for adoption. It has been suggested that *Juno*, which featured a middle-class sixteen-year-old who opts to give her baby up for adoption, made getting pregnant and giving the baby up for adoption seem cool, an experience that can give a floundering teen character and definition, all the while preserving her social and family life without the consequences of becoming a teen parent. Several analysts and writers have worried that *Juno*'s plotline encourages teenage girls to see both pregnancy and adoption in a fashionable and fathomable light.

Sarah S. Brown, CEO of the National Campaign to Prevent Teen and Unplanned Pregnancy, is one person concerned about the message girls will get from *Juno*. In Brown's opinion, the movie irresponsibly paints a portrait of a pregnant teen who has a very support-ive family—a rarity among teens who find themselves pregnant. In the movie, after briefly contemplating her options and visiting an unrealistically portrayed abor-tion clinic, Juno announces to her parents that she is pregnant and will be giving the baby up for adoption. Her parents say once that they think that is a tough thing to do, but then get on board with the idea by cracking jokes and making a plan of action.

While Juno does endure some difficulties as a preg-nant teen—mostly relating to her growing size and the social isolation she feels from her classmates—she is overwhelmingly portrayed as a snarky, upbeat, normal kid who is all too happy to be able to help the infer-tile couple who is interested in adopting her baby. Only briefly at the end of the film—as she lays in bed post-delivery, crying, cradled by her boyfriend—is Juno shown to wrestle with the enormity of her decision or feel any of its weight. When Juno is next seen, she is back to her carefree teenage self, and she and her boyfriend have obviously been brought closer by the experience.

Many are critical of the movie's message that enduring a pregnancy and going through with an adoption can be an overwhelmingly character-building, rather than destructive, experience for a person. As such they have disapproved of the plotline for showing Juno's experience as entirely too easy and improbable. "Adolescents see it through the lens of the 'me generation,'" says Brown. "If the baby got handed off and she got the boyfriend back (as happens in *Juno*), what's the problem?"[1] Gloria Feldt, former president of Planned Parenthood, agrees that *Juno* is short on reality and dangerously overlooks the severe challenges of enduring a pregnancy and giving one's baby up for adoption as a teenager. "I was Juno once—that sixteen year old pregnant girl, and life isn't like that at all," she says. "Juno is an adorable fantasy.... The narrative implies that carrying a pregnancy to term and relinquishing the baby—giving it up for adoption— is nothing. But we know that it isn't so for a pregnant woman. That's totally unrealistic."[2]

Yet others applauded *Juno* for offering teens an alternative to the "have your baby/terminate your baby" dichotomy they are typically presented with. They praise the film for showing teens a strong young role model who takes responsibility for her actions. As one reviewer put it, "Juno is driven by the chance to make her own unconventional choice"[3]—that is, putting the baby up for adoption is a way in which an already unconventional teen can further assert her stray-from-the-pack identity. Gary Hoppenstand, a pop culture professor at Michigan State University, agrees. "Moral issues aside, you have a younger person who got into a situation and, in a sense, is taking responsibility for it and resisting tremendous social pressure," he says. "It's showing a kind of strength and empowerment for the young that older, traditional people will not understand or comprehend."[4] Many Americans agree with Hoppenstand that adoption can be a reasonable choice for a pregnant teen, and one that should be explored more often and regarded with respect.

Whether pregnant teens should consider placing their babies for adoption is one of the many issues explored in *Writing the Critical Essay: Teen Pregnancy*. The causes of teen pregnancy, its related risks, and what laws should be made regulating it are explored in passionately argued viewpoints and model essays. Thought-provoking writing exercises and step-by-step instructions help readers write their own five-paragraph persuasive essays on this compelling and personal subject.

Notes

1. Quoted in Sharon Jayson, "Does 'Juno' Show Strength or Glorify Teen Pregnancy?" *USA Today*, May 27, 2008. www.usatoday.com/news/health/2008-03-09-juno-pregnancy-main-N.htm.
2. Gloria Feldt, interviewed by Linda Lowen in "What 'Juno' Says About Teen Pregnancy, Abortion and Choice: Film Avoids Real Issues and Challenges Faced by Pregnant Teens," About.com, 2007. http://womensissues.about.com/od/teenpregnancy/a/JunoAntiChoice.htm.
3. Ann Hulbert, "*Juno* and the Culture Wars: How the Movie Disarms the Family Values Debate," *Slate*, December 18, 2007. www.slate.com/id/2180275.
4. Quoted in Sharon Jayson, "Does 'Juno' Show Strength or Glorify Teen Pregnancy?"

Section One: Opposing Viewpoints on Teen Pregnancy

Teaching Teens About Birth Control Reduces Teen Pregnancy

Cecile Richards

In the following essay Cecile Richards argues that birth-control-based sex education helps prevent teen pregnancy. Programs that tell kids to wait to have sex have not had any success at reducing the rate of teen pregnancy, she says. Richards believes students need information about contraception so they can be prepared to have safe sex once they decide to become sexually active. She concludes that teens cannot avoid pregnancy if they are not taught about birth control. They should be encouraged to wait as long as possible, but they must be taught about birth control so they can protect themselves from pregnancy when they do decide to have sex.

Richards is president of the Planned Parenthood Federation of America.

Consider the following questions:

1. What percent of U.S. births does Richards say are to teens?
2. What was the conclusion of more than 115 studies that probed the effectiveness of abstinence-only education?
3. How much money does Richards say has been wasted on abstinence-only programs?

There was Juno. There was Gloucester.[1] There was Jamie Lynn Spears. And now, once again teen pregnancy has captured the attention of the media all across the country. Unfortunately, the media hype glamorizes an issue that is anything but glamorous.

As the mother of two teenagers, I recognize the real struggles families face keeping their kids healthy and safe.

Teen Pregnancy Is a Serious Problem

Teen pregnancy happens to hundreds of thousands of girls each year from Bangor to San Antonio to Fresno. And, for the vast majority of these teens, the pregnancy was not planned. Most of these teens find themselves unexpectedly pregnant without the financial—or familial—resources to become a parent.

At Planned Parenthood health centers across the country, we see these teens, and their families, every single day. Last year [2007], we [Planned Parenthood] provided sexuality education to 1.2 million teens and adults. And we see firsthand their struggle—their struggle to stay healthy, to make responsible decisions, to succeed in life.

This year alone, it is estimated that 750,000 teenage girls in the U.S. will become pregnant. That is more than 12 times the number of people diagnosed with AIDS in 2008 and more than the total number of people expected to die from some type of cancer this year. Put another way, 11 percent of all U.S. births are to teens.

Pregnancy Puts Teens at Risk

What do these numbers tell us? First, whether we approve or not, our teens are having sex. By the time they turn 19, seven in ten teenagers have had sex at least once. And second, it tells us that when they have sex, they are not using protection.

1. The author is referring to Gloucester, Massachusetts, where several high school students made a pact to get pregnant together during the 2007–2008 school year.

Actress Ellen Page received many awards for her portrayal of a pregnant teen in the film Juno. *Critics of the movie's content believe it glamorized teen pregnancy.*

But there's more: Pregnancy isn't the only consequence. According to the federal Centers for Disease Control and Prevention, one in four teen girls has a sexually transmitted infection. The consequences of their actions can follow them for a lifetime. If that does not constitute a public health crisis, I don't know what does.

As parents, as a country, we don't want our kids to become parents when they aren't finished being children themselves. America's teenage girls and boys should be allowed to have their childhood; there is more than enough time for them in the future to bear the other responsibilities of adulthood and be parents. Parenting is too important to be left to chance. And the fact is that it doesn't have to be.

We Must Arm Teens with Knowlege

Sexuality education for teens that is founded on medically accurate information, that is abstinence-based but also teaches contraception, has been proven to be effective in preventing unintended pregnancies. Teaching our teens about sex isn't what makes them have or not have sex. Teaching our teens about sex is how they learn about prevention. It's how they learn to protect themselves from sexually transmitted infection and disease. It's how they learn to stay safe. Sexuality education works to reduce teen pregnancies. It works to help reduce the transmission of sexually transmitted infections. And it works to help keep teens healthy and help enable them to plan healthy families.

A National Campaign to Prevent Teen and Unplanned Pregnancy analysis of more than 115 studies conducted to measure the effectiveness of teen education programs found that abstinence-only programs did not help our teens to abstain or delay the age at which they had sex.

> ## Teens Need to Know About Contraception
>
> [Abstinence-only supporters] still insist that American children should be deprived of sex education, lied to about contraception and maintained in a state of medieval ignorance. If their own children end up with syphilis or unwanted babies, that, it seems, is a price they will pay for preserving their beliefs.
>
> George Monbiot, "These Denialogues Don't Care If Their Own Children End Up with Syphilis," *Guardian* (Manchester, UK), July 27, 2009.

Sex Education Helps Teens Avoid Pregnancy

Planned Parenthood educators teach teens and their parents to become smart about sexuality, and about how to talk to each other about sexual and reproductive health. We have peer educator programs that train teens to talk

Teen Birthrates and Abstinence-Only Funding in the United States

Shown are the states with the top ten birthrates. These states have also received large amounts of federal funding for abstinence-only education programs. Compare this to the states with the ten lowest teen birthrates, many of which received small or no amounts of federal funding for abstinence-only education programs. Critics say this shows abstinence-only education does not prevent teen pregnancy.

Highest Teen Birthrate States

State	Birthrate	Amount of Federal Funding Received for Abstinence-Only Programs, 2008.
Mississippi	1	$5,742,594
New Mexico	2	$1,349,883
Texas	3	$14,289,087
Arkansas	4	$4,030,124
Arizona	5	$5,185,998
Oklahoma	6	$1,289,869
Nevada	7	$851,532
Tennessee	8	$5,668,444
Kentucky	9	$3,566,720
Georgia	10	$12,282,363

Lowest Teen Birthrate States

State	Birthrate	Amount of Federal Funding Received for Abstinence-Only Programs, 2008.
Minnesota	42	$0
Rhode Island	43	$0
North Dakota	44	$88,991
Maine	45	$165,000
New York	46	$7,560,885
New Jersey	47	$4,079,835
Connecticut	48	$599,800
Massachusetts	49	$1,409,826
Vermont	50	$0
New Hampshire	51	$94,901

Taken from: Centers for Disease Control and Prevention, The Pew Forum on Religion and Public Life, Sexuality Information and Education Council of the United States (SIECUS), 2008.

hools
ut
?

ABSTINENCE-PLUS
3.6%

NOTHING
2.3%

ABSTINENCE-ONLY
94%

Texas Freedom Network Education Fund speaker Kathy Miller announces the release of a study that shows Texas is failing families and teens when it comes to sex education.

to their peers about sexual health. At some of our health centers, we offer special "teen only" hours to help make teens comfortable and welcome. We sponsor parent-teen nights to help facilitate open, honest and full communication between teens and their parents. We have programs targeted at parents to help give them the skills, resources and confidence they need to talk to their children. And, we have programs for pregnant and parenting teens that provide a supportive environment and skills training to cope with the challenges of parenthood and adolescence.

For the past eight years, more than $1.5 billion of taxpayers' money has been wasted on abstinence-only programs that don't work. There is a lot at stake right now for American teenagers. These policies must change with the [Obama] administration. When it comes to sexuality education, there should be no debate. The only way our children can be prepared is to be informed; this isn't about ideology, it's about the health and safety of our kids.

Analyze the essay:

1. Richards uses history, facts, and examples to make her argument that teaching teens about birth control can reduce teen pregnancy. She does not, however, use any quotations to support her point. If you were to rewrite this essay and insert quotations, what authorities might you quote from? Where would you place these quotes?

2. Richards is the president of Planned Parenthood, a nationwide organization that works to prevent unintended pregnancies and champions the right of women to make informed decisions about pregnancy. Does knowing her background influence your opinion of her argument? In what way?

Teaching Students About Abstinence Reduces Teen Pregnancy

Katherine Bradley and Christine Kim

Teaching students to abstain from sex is the best way to reduce teen pregnancy, argue Katherine Bradley and Christine Kim in the following essay. They think that teaching teens about birth control just encourages them to have premarital sex. Furthermore, birth control is not foolproof—even when teens use them properly, condoms fail and teens can still get pregnant. The only surefire way to avoid pregnancy is to not have sex—and this is what the authors think should be taught to American teens. They oppose budget cuts that plan to eliminate abstinence education programs, arguing that kids need to know they have the option to abstain from sex entirely.

Bradley is a visiting fellow in the Center for Religion and Civil Society. Kim is an analyst with the Heritage Foundation, a conservative research organization.

Consider the following questions:

1. What were the findings of a 2008 Heritage report, according to the authors?
2. What percent of parents do the authors say want their children taught that abstaining from sex is best?
3. What percent of parents think contraception should receive more emphasis than abstinence, according to the authors?

Katherine Bradley and Christine Kim, "The Case for Maintaining Abstinence Education Funding," *Abstinence & Marriage Education Partnership*, on Web Memo #2562, July, 24, 2009. Reproduced by permission of the Heritage Foundation.

The President's budget for Fiscal Year 2010 would eliminate abstinence education funding. The [Barack] Obama Administration has instead requested the creation of yet another comprehensive sex education program, the "Teen Pregnancy Prevention" program. The House of Representatives has included this request in their annual appropriations bill that is now moving through Congress.

According to the Department of Health and Human Services (HHS), in FY [fiscal year] 2008, HHS spent $4 on programs that promote "safe sex" and contraception to teens for every $1 spent on abstinence education. Congress should resist the President's request to fund another comprehensive sex education program for teens and instead maintain abstinence education.

The push to reduce teen pregnancy goes hand-in-hand with abstinence says Taylor Moore, eighteen, as she speaks to teenagers and their parents at Salem Baptist Church in Champaign, Illinois.

The Push to Reduce Teen Pregnancy

The 1996 welfare reform bill placed a renewed focus on reducing the number of out-of-wedlock births and teen pregnancies. Abstinence education funding was included in this legislation to help accomplish this important mission. Organizations receiving grants from this program were committed to teaching "the social, psychological and health gains from abstaining from sexual activity" and that "abstinence from sexual activity is the only certain way to avoid out-of-wedlock pregnancy, sexually transmitted disease (STDs), and other associated health problems."

According to the Centers for Disease Control, between 1995 and 2002, the out-of-wedlock birthrate for teens ages 15–17 years old dropped an astonishing 30 percent and 12 percent for teens ages 18–19. However, over more recent years the rate for 18–19 year olds has increased slightly by 5 percent, indicating that a renewed focus should be given to reaching this population.

> ## Abstinence-Centered Education Can Work
>
> Emerging evidence supports the notion that abstinence-centered strategies, if well-designed and implemented, can significantly and substantially reduce teen sexual initiation for periods of 1 to 2 years and thereby may positively impact the health of American adolescents.
>
> Stan Weed, testimony before the U.S. House of Representatives Committee on Oversight and Government Reform, April 23, 2008. http://oversight.house.gov/documents/20080423114651.pdf.

Abstinence Programs Reduce and Delay Teen Sex

Studies have shown that abstinence-based programs have effectively reduced sexual activity and delayed the initiation of sexual activity. For example, the latest evaluation, which examined seventh graders in northern Virginia, reported that, one year after the program, students who received abstinence education were half as likely as non-participants to initiate sexual activity. This result accounted for the existing background differences between program participants and non-participants. That is, the evaluation compared near-identical students except for their participation in the abstinence education program.

A 2008 Heritage report analyzed 21 different studies done on abstinence-based education programs. It found that in 16 of the 21 reports there were statistically significant positive results in delaying early sexual activity and initiation. Of these studies, 15 examined abstinence programs whose primary message was teaching abstinence, while six of the studies were on virginity pledge programs. Of the virginity pledge programs, five reported positive findings.

Abstaining Has Many Benefits

The research also suggests that teens who remain abstinent have higher academic achievement. Analyzing a large nationally representative sample of youths, a Heritage study found that compared to sexually active teens, those who remained abstinent through high school were 60 percent less likely to be expelled from school, 50 percent less likely to drop out of high school, and almost twice as likely to graduate from college.

Abstinent teens also report better psychological well-being than their peers who are sexually active, and girls, in particular, appear to benefit from delayed sexual activity. Reduced sexual activity decreases teen exposure to sexually transmitted diseases (STDs), reduces their risks of having children out of wedlock, and improves their emotional and mental health.

Parental Support for Abstinence Education

A Zogby poll in December 2003 found that 96 percent of parents said they want teenagers to be taught that abstinence is best. Seventy-nine percent said they want young people taught that sex should be reserved for marriage or in an adult relationship leading to marriage. In addition, the poll showed that "93 percent of parents want teens taught that the younger the age an individual begins sexual activity, the more likely he or she is to be

A 2007 Zogby poll explained to parents what abstinence education programs consist of. Then it asked how they preferred their child be educated. The majority said abstinence.

Question: Would you rather your child be educated in Comprehensive Sex Education courses, or in Abstinence Education courses?

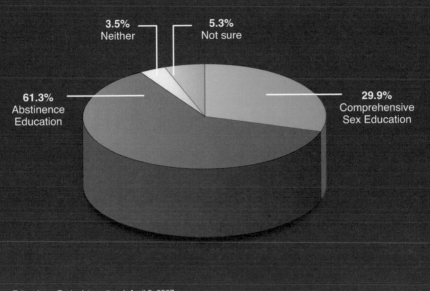

3.5% Neither

5.3% Not sure

61.3% Abstinence Education

29.9% Comprehensive Sex Education

Taken from: Zogby International, April 5, 2007.

infected by STDs, to have an abortion, and to give birth out of wedlock."

These are all themes and messages woven throughout abstinence education programs. Teens are taught about all of the possible consequences of engaging in sexual activity, including the risks of contracting a STD, heightened chances of depression, lower academic achievement and greater chances of teen pregnancy and out-of-wedlock childbearing. They teach life and relationship skills and help lay the foundation for personal responsibility.

Comprehensive sex education programs often claim they include a message of abstinence. However, the manner in which it is presented is often downplayed and given little attention or focus. These programs do not focus on teaching personal responsibility, building character, or developing strong decision-making skills. Instead they presume teen sexual activity and convey that protected sex is a safe and acceptable alternative to abstinence. The Zogby poll found that only 7 percent of parents think the message of contraception should receive more emphasis than abstinence.

It Just Plain Works

Abstinence education equips today's youth with the knowledge of the positive benefits of delaying sexual activity and decision-making skills to help them achieve their future goals. Before cutting federal funding for abstinence education programs, policymakers should revisit the original argument for supporting abstinence education—reducing rising teen pregnancy and unwed births—and consider all of the evidence that indicates its effectiveness.

Analyze the essay:

1. Bradley and Kim suggest that teens who abstain from sex are more likely to stay in school and graduate from college. How do you think Cecile Richards, author of the previous essay, would respond to this claim?
2. Think about the teens at your school. Which do you think would benefit them more—a sex education based on abstinence messages or one that teaches them about birth control? Why?

Giving Teens Emergency Contraception Can Prevent Teen Pregnancy

Lisa Waller and William Bryson

In the following essay Lisa Waller and William Bryson argue that emergency contraception (EC) can prevent a significant number of unintended teen pregnancies. They explain that EC is similar to birth control pills—it uses the same kinds of safe hormones to prevent pregnancy by disrupting the implantation of a fertilized egg in the uterus. They cite studies that found when teens were given information about EC, or given EC itself, pregnancy rates went down, but teens seemed no more likely to have unprotected sex or to contract sexually transmitted diseases. Unfortunately, say the authors, most teens are unaware of EC or do not know where to get it. Waller and Bryson conclude that emergency contraception can be a powerful tool in the fight against teen pregnancy and teens should have greater access to it.

Waller is a health care professional who practices in Atlanta, Georgia. Bryson teaches at the Emory University School of Medicine.

Consider the following questions:

1. What percent of unintended pregnancies do the authors say emergency contraception could prevent?
2. What did a study of African American youth find about what happens when teens receive education about EC or both education and EC itself?
3. Name at least three organizations who think emergency contraception should be a key component of pregnancy prevention efforts.

Lisa Waller and William Bryson, "Can Emergency Contraception Help to Reduce Teen Pregnancy?" *Journal of the American Academy of Physician Assistants*, vol. 20, June 2007, pp. 42-48. Copyright © 2007 Haymarket Business Publications Ltd. Used with permission of Haymarket Media, conveyed through Copyright Clearance Center, Inc.

Health professionals agree that the numbers of teenage pregnancies and termination rates are too high, but reducing the high rates of adolescent pregnancy continues to be a challenge for clinicians. Emergency contraception (EC) has the potential to prevent 75% to 85% of unintended pregnancies and to eliminate approximately 50,000 elective abortions per year. In an adolescent patient population where contraception compliance is a serious issue, EC should be supported as an essential component to pregnancy prevention.

Free Emergency Contraceptives (EC) are given out by a Planned Parenthood representitive of Northern New England as part of the organization's FREE Emergency Contraceptive Day, in hopes of reducing teen pregnancy.

How EC Works

The same hormones found in oral contraceptives (OCs) are used for EC. When taken in a concentrated dose within 72 hours of unprotected intercourse, EC can prevent pregnancy. Studies have shown a potential benefit at more than 120 hours postintercourse, but FDA [Food and Drug Administration] guidelines for approved use specify a maximum of 72 hours. . . .

EC is ineffective if a fertilized egg has successfully implanted within the uterine wall.

EC Is Perfectly Safe

The hormones in EC have been used in OCs taken by millions of women for decades. Serious complication rates, which are related to the estrogen component, have been proven to be extremely low. There is no associated toxicity with hormone use, so there is little danger in inadvertent overdose. There are no addictive properties to the hormones. In fact, the side effects—such as menstrual irregularities and nausea—may actually discourage women from using EC repeatedly. There have been no deaths or other serious consequences of an acute overdose of EC hormones. Decades of research show no risk of hormone exposure if a pregnancy has already been established. . . .

EC Prevents Pregnancy Without Raising STD or Unprotected Sex Rates

[M.A.] Gold and Colleagues conducted a randomized prospective study comparing a cohort [group] of adolescents who received EC education and a single dose of EC to be used if needed to a group receiving EC education alone. Researchers told those provided with education alone that EC would be available to them through the clinic if needed. The aim of the study was to ascertain whether providing EC in advance would lead to higher sexual and contraceptive risk-taking. Subjects were predominately African-American, with a mean age of 17.1

Emergency Contraception Can Prevent Unwanted Pregnancy

Studies show that if one hundred women each had sex once during the fertile period of their menstrual cycle but did not use contraception, eight would likely become pregnant. But if one hundred women used emergency contraception pills, only a couple would likely become pregnant. This is why supporters say that EC can be a powerful tool in the fight against teen pregnancy.

Effectiveness of Emergency Contraceptive Pills (ECPs)

If 100 woman each had unprotected sex once during the second or third week of their menstrual cycle...

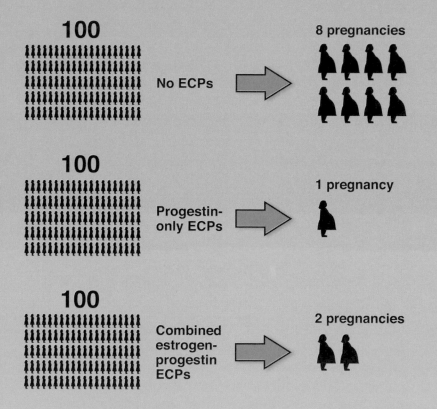

100

No ECPs

8 pregnancies

100

Progestin-only ECPs

1 pregnancy

100

Combined estrogen-progestin ECPs

2 pregnancies

Taken from: Information & Knowledge for Optimal Health (INFO) Project, Johns Hopkins Bloomberg School of Public Health.

years; nearly half were Medicaid recipients. A 6-month follow-up showed that providing EC in advance facilitates its earlier use and decreases overall pregnancy rates. Advance EC provision had no negative influence on the teenagers' use of routine contraceptive methods. In addition, there were no more sexually transmitted infections or rates of unprotected intercourse among EC users as compared to controls.

[T.] Raine and colleagues completed a controlled trial of female participants aged 16 to 24 years, 76% of whom were members of an ethnic minority, who attended a publicly-funded family planning clinic. About half had been pregnant before. As with the Gold study, patients were assigned to receive EC education and a single dose of EC in advance or education alone. Researchers found that advance provision of EC was the strongest predictor of EC use, after controlling for contraceptive method, pattern of contraceptive use, and frequency of unprotected sex. There was no significant increase in unprotected intercourse. Increased knowledge alone, without advance medication supply, did not increase requests for EC or promote behavior change. . . .

> ## Why Teens Need Access to Emergency Contraception
>
> It's not as if adolescent females are going to say to themselves, "Oh, I'll just use Plan B as my only form of birth control." Not when it costs $40 a pop. . . . But making it easier to obtain will help prevent unwanted pregnancies for girls who were having sex when the condom slipped or broke; for girls who forgot to take their contraception; and, particularly, for girls who were coerced into having unprotected sex, or were raped.
>
> Maura Kelly, "Plan B Should Be an Option for All: The Morning-After Pill Should Be Made Available Without a Prescription to All Girls, Regardless of Age," *Guardian* (Manchester, UK), March 31, 2009.

Access to Emergency Contraception Should Be Improved

The American Academy of Pediatrics, the Society for Adolescent Medicine, the AAPA [American Academy of Physician Assistants], and the American Medical Association have issued position or policy statements in support of EC as an essential component of both primary and secondary pregnancy prevention efforts. However, despite established guidelines for its use, low levels of EC prescribing and discussion persist throughout the United States. In an attempt to understand the low utilization despite demonstrated safety and efficacy, we must address several real or perceived barriers.

Reducing the high rates of adolescent pregnancy continues to be a challenge for clinicians. In 1996, the Kaiser Foundation in association with Princeton Survey Research Associates conducted telephone interviews on teenagers' perceptions about sexual activity, pregnancy, contraception, and sources of information about sex and birth control. Of the 757 girls and 753 boys interviewed, less than 25% of either gender knew that "anything could be done" after unprotected sex to prevent pregnancy. Teenage females were slightly more aware than were males of the terms *emergency contraception* or *morning-after pill* (33% versus 24%). If they were aware, very few understood that a prescription is required or that there is a limited time in which to take EC. Knowledge was highest among older, white adolescents. Upon learning about EC, two thirds of the teenage girls reported they would be likely to use it. The reasons cited for not using EC were the lack of a regular medical provider and the need to share sensitive information with a provider. An interesting contrast is the higher knowledge level of EC among European youth: 75% to 95% in both males and females. . . .

EC Has Helped Reduce Unplanned Pregnancy in Europe

Historically, women in the United States have had fewer contraceptive options than women in most other developed countries. EC is widely available throughout Europe. Since 1999, France has made EC available without a prescription through pharmacists, with a large portion of the expense reimbursed through the national health plan. In 2000, the laws changed to allow high school nurses to distribute EC. French pharmacies now dispense EC at no cost, without parental approval, to adolescents.

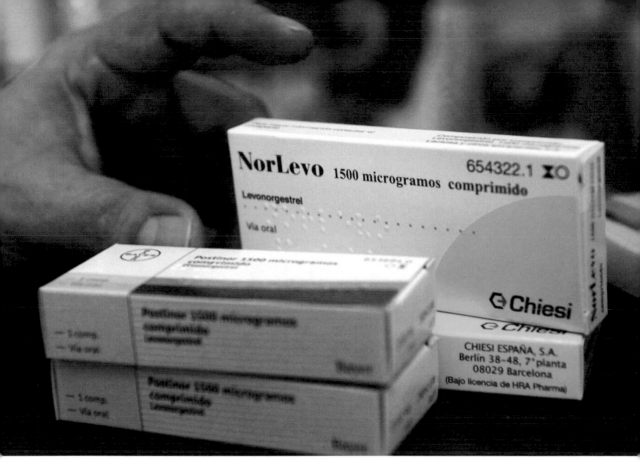

Pharmacists must counsel consumers about its use and give information about alternative forms of routine birth control. In this way pharmacists can serve as an entry-point into the health care system for adolescents. By having access to lists of referring primary care sites, they are able to link adolescents to reproductive health care services. France is a model worth studying, as their abortion rates are some of the lowest in the world. . . .

Widespread availability of postcoital contraception remains one of the most promising ways to reduce this country's high rates of unplanned pregnancies and abortions. In a population of patients for whom consistent contraceptive use is seemingly impossible, PAs [physician assistants] should address pregnancy risk reduction as part of adolescent practice, regardless of the patient's gender. PAs should familiarize themselves with EC in order to feel comfortable prescribing it and should be

The emergency contraceptive pill has been available without a doctor's prescription throughout pharamacies in Spain since September 28, 2009.

knowledgeable about EC availability and protocols for dispensing. . . .

It is crucial to reiterate messages regarding safe sexual practices and to reinforce condom usage, as the rates of STIs [sexually transmitted infections] are still too high. Present EC as a true *emergency* method and not one to be used routinely. And no matter how sexually experienced the patient is, it is always worthwhile to suggest to adolescents the value of abstinence.

Analyze the essay:

1. Waller and Bryson are both health care professionals. Does knowing their background influence your opinion of their support for emergency contraception? Why or why not?

2. Waller and Bryson describe how EC works, saying it prevents unintended pregnancies and thus the need for teens to get abortions. How do you think Teens for Life, the author of the following essay, would respond to this claim? Cite from both essays in your answer.

Teens Should Not Have Access to Emergency Contraception

Teens for Life

Teens for Life is a conservative pro-life group that seeks to instill in teens a respect for life. In the following essay, it argues that emergency contraception is too dangerous to give to teens. The group contends that EC causes an abortion to take place because it disrupts the natural course of a fertilized egg. From this perspective, EC is an abortion drug, but teens take it without realizing this aspect of it. EC contains high levels of hormones that Teens for Life says can have dangerous side effects when used without supervision. The group also says countries that give their teens access to EC experience high rates of sexually transmitted diseases, because kids consider having access to EC an excuse not to use any birth control. For these and other reasons, Teens for Life says emergency contraception should not be given to teens.

Consider the following questions:

1. In what way does the author think sexual predators could use EC to their advantage?
2. What does the author say has been the United Kingdom's experience with the emergency contraception called Plan B?
3. What does the word "semantics" mean in the context of the essay?

"Speak Out: Emergency Contraception," Teens For Life (teensforlife.com), 2009.
Reproduced by permission.

"Emergency Contraception" (EC) is the term applied to a very high dosage of hormones (40 to 50 times stronger than a daily "birth control" pill) taken within 72 hours of unprotected sexual activity. Proponents of EC claim it will prevent unintended pregnancy, but if fertilization has occurred prior to using EC, it will cause the abortion of a human embryo.

EC Causes an Early Abortion

There are three possible ways that EC can work:

1. It can prevent ovulation (the release of the unfertilized egg cell from the ovary). Without ovulation, there is no egg to be fertilized and pregnancy is avoided.
2. It can prevent fertilization.
3. It can prevent implantation of the new developing human embryo in the lining of the uterus. In other words, it can cause an early abortion.

Supporters of EC repeatedly deny that it will cause an early abortion, but that position flies against established medical fact. EC supporters who deny its abortion-causing action do so by redefining when human life begins. In other words, they reject the scientific fact that human life begins with the union of the sperm and the egg (fertilization) and claim that conception occurs only when the tiny human embryo implants in the uterine wall (implantation).

Many Reasons to Be Concerned

EC in no way stops or protects against the transmission of sexually transmitted diseases [STDs]. It is not a "magic pill" that makes the consequences of sexual activity go away—and those consequences often include STDs that will be with you for life.

Users of the drug are not being properly informed about the potential abortifacient action of the drug. If this drug is taken after fertilization has occurred, but before the newly formed human embryo implants in the uterine wall, it will cause an early abortion by blocking the embryo from implantation.

Numerous reports from countries where EC has been used for some time, that EC has little or no statistical impact on pregnancy or abortion rates. In fact, one study from the UK shows that abortion rates have risen with widespread distribution of EC.

Bad for Pharmacists, Good for Sexual Predators

EC places pharmacists under fire. Pharmacists across the country are quickly finding that new abortion-causing drugs are placing them squarely on the front lines of

Pharmacist Rich Quayle, 54, is one of the pharmacists from Walgreens in Illinois that was placed on indefinite unpaid leave for refusing to dispense the morning-after pill due to religious and ethical grounds.

the abortion debate. In Southern Illinois, for example, four pharmacists were recently forced to file a lawsuit after being placed on unpaid leave by Walgreens when they refused to violate their personal consciences by dispensing so-called "morning-after" pills. Walgreens officials claim they were forced into the action because of an executive order by [then] Illinois Governor Rod Blagojevich that demands that all pharmacists in the state fill all prescriptions, even if it's a prescription for an abortion-causing drug.

Sexual predators will rely on EC to "cover their tracks". Easy over-the-counter access to EC is a sexual predator's dream come true and will lead to intense pressure on young girls by older boys and men to use EC, claiming that it will remove any consequences of sexual activity.

> ## Emergency Contraception Is Too Dangerous for Teens to Get Without Their Parents' Permission
>
> **Birth control pills require a doctor's prescription, but a drug that is more powerful doesn't? . . . In most states, minors can't get a tattoo, body piercings or go to a tanning salon without a parent's permission, but we are going to leave them alone to take Plan B. . . . This is not what is best for our daughters.**
>
> Mike Galanos, "Plan B Risky for 17-Year-Old Girls," CNN.com, May 1, 2009.

The EC Pill Has Significant Health Risks

EC carries none of the counseling safeguards that normal birth control pills require. Birth control pills are available by prescription only for sound medical reasons: They can cause significant or life-threatening conditions such as blood clots and heart attacks. Birth control pills are contraindicated for women with diabetes, liver problems, heart disease, breast cancer, deep vein thrombosis, and for women who smoke and are over 35. A medical exam is necessary to ensure that none of these contraindications exists. For example, according to the Centers for Disease Control, approximately 1.85 million women of reproductive age (18–44) have diabetes; approximately 500,000 do not know that they have the disease. By contrast, users of EC are not required to have a medical exam or any of the common sense safeguards.

Lack of scientific studies examining risks. There is a clear lack of scientific studies on the long-term-effects of Plan B [a brand of emergency contraception] with respect to high dosage and repeated use in both women and adolescents. While the patient package directions on Plan B state it is not to be used more than twice a month, the directions and promotions of Plan B state it is also to be used in emergencies. These emergencies include unprotected sex and the failure of other birth control devices—factors that may arise more than twice a month.

EC Increases STD Rates
STD rates have skyrocketed in countries where Plan B has been deregulated. Since becoming available in the United

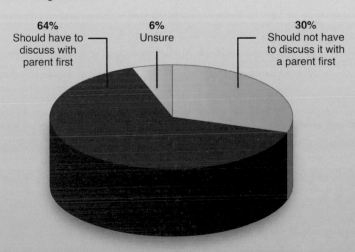

Teens Should Not Have Over-the-Counter Access to EC Without Parental Consent

In 2009 the Food and Drug Administration made it legal for seventeen-year-olds to get emergency contraception pills over-the-counter without a prescription. But the majority of Americans think teens should have to consult with a parent before doing so.

64% Should have to discuss with parent first

6% Unsure

30% Should not have to discuss it with a parent first

Taken from: Rasmussen Reports, May 5, 2009.

Pro-choice demonstrators protest the ban on the distribution of free 'morning-after' pills in Chile. The Chilean congress argues that the emergency contraceptive constitutes abortion, which is illegal in Chile under all circumstances.

Kingdom in 2001, Plan B usage among teenage girls has more than doubled. STDs with sharp increases include chlamydia and gonorrhea, with the highest increases in 16 to 19 year olds. Because STDs such as chlamydia can cause infertility in women, the impact that increased access to and usage of Plan B has on STD rates could have a direct causal relationship to increased future infertility rates of U.S. women.

Link of Plan B to ectopic pregnancy. Statements from the World Health Organization and leading medical officials taken together provide a warning that increased risk of ectopic pregnancy [when the fertilized egg implants outside the uterus] exists with Plan B usage. Additionally, common physical side-effects a woman experiences following Plan B usage often mimic ectopic pregnancy symptoms, including cramping and severe pain. Consequently, there is valid concern for Plan B usage to actually mask ectopic pregnancy, an acute, life-threatening condition.

The Truth About EC

Supporters of emergency contraception are playing semantics with the language, and that is why they are so deceptive. This is a decades-old controversy. Until the mid-1960's it was universally accepted that fertilization was the beginning of pregnancy. Under political pressure intended to accommodate abortion-causing drugs, a new definition of pregnancy moved the beginning of pregnancy from fertilization to implantation, but the semantics do nothing to change medical fact—physical human life begins at the point when a human egg is fertilized by a human sperm. At that point, a unique human being has been created that will continue to develop until birth unless that process is interrupted by a spontaneous miscarriage or an abortion.

It will take approximately 7 to 10 days for the newly formed human embryo to implant in the uterine wall. If that human embryo is prevented from implantation through the use of a drug like an emergency contraceptive, it is being aborted.

Analyze the essay:

1. Teens for Life says emergency contraception encourages teens to have unprotected sex and thus increases the rates of sexually transmitted diseases. How do you think Waller and Bryson, authors of the previous essay, would respond to this claim?

2. Teens for Life characterizes emergency contraception as an abortion drug. Waller and Bryon characterize emergency contraception as a tool to help prevent abortion. After reading both essays, with which authors do you agree? Does EC qualify as an abortion drug in your opinion? Or, can its use help prevent the need for abortions? Explain your answer using evidence from the texts.

Pregnant Teens Should Need Parental Permission to Get an Abortion

National Right to Life Educational Trust Fund

In the following essay the National Right to Life Educational Trust Fund argues that parents should have the legal right to be involved in their teen's decision to have an abortion. The author says that abortion is too risky a procedure to let a teen deal with on her own—the surgery can cause medical and psychological problems that can haunt a person for life. When faced with one of the most important decisions of her whole life, the author says, it is critical for a teen to consult with her parents. This is why the Supreme Court has upheld the legality of parental involvement laws and why the majority of Americans support them. For all these reasons, the author supports laws that make it necessary for a teen to either notify her parents or get her parents' permission before she has an abortion.

The National Right to Life Educational Trust Fund is a pro-life group that opposes abortion.

A complete version of the original document with footnoted citations for the facts and studies mentioned is available at www.nrlc.org/Factsheets/FS17_Teens andAbortion.pdf.

Consider the following questions:

1. According to the author, what are the consequences of secret teen abortions?
2. What does the author say Texas experienced after instituting a parental notification law in 2000?
3. What percent of Americans support parental consent laws, according to the author?

"Teens & Abortion: Why Parents Should Know," National Right to Life Educational Trust Fund, May 2006. Reproduced by permission.

It is simply a fact that adolescents develop physically before fully maturing psychologically and socially. While adolescents are physically capable of having children, at this point in their psychological development they are more likely to follow their immediate emotional responses than to rationally consider their options and their long term consequences.

Teens Need Their Parents When Pregnant

A teen's biggest concern may be avoiding discovery by her parents or peers or trying to hold onto her boyfriend rather than determining how the birth or abortion of the child may affect the rest of her life.

Teens tend to rely on others when making decisions, a healthy pattern when those influencing a teen have her own best interests at heart, but an area of concern in situations where the young teens can be exploited by older individuals, such as boyfriends or abortion clinic counselors, who teens view as more experienced and knowledgeable, but may not recognize as having their own agendas.

Abortion Is Too Risky to Face Alone

There are physical, social and psychological consequences of abortion, and these may be worse for teens. Anyone having a surgical or chemical abortion may face complications such as perforation, scarring, hemorrhaging, infection, or even death. Women who abort run higher risks of future infertility, miscarriages, ectopic pregnancy, and premature birth of future children. For teens, abortion may mean never being able to have children.

Abortion is an identified risk factor in breast cancer. The risk for aborting teens may be even greater, especially since they are not likely to have reaped the protective effect of previously giving birth.

Women who have abortions are also at a higher risk of psychological and social problems, including drug

Pregnant teens are often worried that their parents or peers will discover their difficult secret.

and alcohol abuse, increased sexual promiscuity, and depression. This is particularly true for teens, as secret abortions create a psychological burden for adolescent girls and can hurt future relationships. Studies also find adolescent suicides one year after an abortion to be significantly higher than adolescent suicide after childbirth.

Parental Involvement Laws Keep Kids Safe

Parental involvement laws are effective. Even while the decline in national abortion rates showed signs of slowing, an extensive study of nearly 400,000 teen pregnancies in Texas showed a significant drop in both abortion and birth rates among minors once a parental notification law went into effect there in 2000. Other studies have shown that states adopting parental involvement laws see abortions drop more than those which don't.

Parental involvement laws are constitutional. In 1976, the Supreme Court decided in *Planned Parenthood of Central Missouri v. Danforth* that states could require the consent of one parent before a minor could have an abortion as long as the law contained a "judicial bypass." Conditions of the bypass were outlined in *Bellotti v. Baird (II)* in 1979, which said the teen could abort without parental consent if she demonstrated her maturity to a judge or if the judge decided an abortion would somehow be in her best interest.

Americans Support Parental Consent Laws

The majority of Americans have favored laws that require pregnant teens to get their parents' permission in order to get an abortion.

"Do you favor or oppose a law requiring women under 18 to get parental consent for any abortion?"

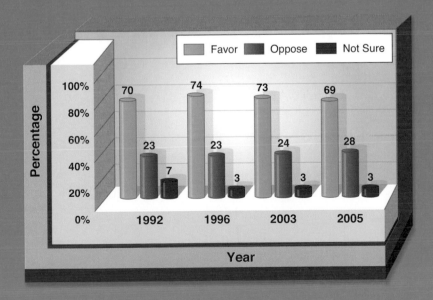

Parental notification was first addressed in 1981 in *H.L. v. Matheson*, which permitted a Utah law requiring abortionists to notify the parents of minors still living at home as a dependent when an abortion is scheduled.

The Court has reaffirmed its decisions on parental involvement several times, most recently *Planned Parenthood v. Casey*, which in 1992 reaffirmed the "central holding" of *Roe*, but in a 7-2 vote explicitly allowed a requirement for one-parent consent with judicial bypass.

The state of California proposed a constitutional amendment that would require doctors to give parents or guardians written notice 48 hours before performing an abortion on a minor.

This decision left parental involvement laws constitutional, provided they have the judicial bypass and exceptions for the life of the mother.

Parental Involvement Is Popular Among All Americans

Even "pro-choice" Americans support parental involvement. Polling consistently shows widespread, popular support for laws requiring that parents be involved in an adolescent's decision to have an abortion. A recent poll showed 72% of the public supported parental consent, and 78% supported parental notification—including 64% of "pro-choice" respondents. Other polling shows support as high as 83%, and as of July 2005, according to PollingReport.com, no poll showed support below 70%.

Parents can help their daughters counter pressures and make informed decisions. No matter what her decision about her unborn child is, a teen's parents can provide their daughter with critical emotional and material support. Not surprisingly, one study found 89% of minors reported they were happier for having told their parents.

> ### Parental Involvement Laws Protect Pregnant Teens
>
> [Do we want] girls going to free-standing abortion clinics for serious medical procedures by doctors they have never seen before—without anyone in their families even knowing[?] . . . Healthcare professionals know that young teens are safest when a parent is involved in their medical care. That's why [it is common sense to] require that a doctor notify a parent or, in case of parental abuse, another adult family member before performing a serious medical procedure on a minor.
>
> Katie Short, "Planned Parenthood Plays Loose with Research," *Los Angeles Times*, October 22, 2008.

Parents Need to Be Involved

Parents can empower adolescent mothers to make pro-life choices by helping raise the child so the minor can still attend school or pursue a career, by offering financial support to raise the child, or by helping their daughter understand and explore the adoption option.

Even if a decision is made to have an abortion, parents can help their children through the tough physical challenges and emotional issues that follow. At the clinic parents can help teens through medical crises by being an important resource about family medical history, which can help determine if certain abortion methods pose special risks for the teen mother.

While many women don't follow up their abortions with doctor visits that can spot deadly complications, teenagers are notorious for "no-showing." Involved, knowledgeable parents are able to take their daughters back to the doctor, and can watch for red flag warnings of depression, drug use, and excessive bleeding that can follow an abortion and signal more serious problems.

Analyze the essay:
1. National Right to Life says that teens need to talk to their parents when facing the problem of pregnancy. Do you think a law is the right way to go about encouraging pregnant teens to talk to their parents? Why or why not?
2. This essay used facts and statistics to help convince you of a certain perspective. Which of these facts or statistics did you find most compelling? Which did you find least compelling? Why?

Pregnant Teens Should Not Need Parental Permission to Get an Abortion

Bixby Center for Global Reproductive Health

In the following essay the Bixby Center for Global Reproductive Health opposes laws that would require pregnant teens to notify their parents or get their parents' permission to have an abortion. The author says the majority of teens are talking to their parents about abortion without being forced to by law. The teens who do not talk to their parents have a valid reason for not doing so—such as they fear being beaten or kicked out of the house. The Bixby Center says such laws put teens at risk for waiting to have abortions (which makes the procedure more dangerous) or for running away from home to a state without such a law. Some teens might even try to give themselves abortions to avoid telling their parents, which could result in death. For all these reasons, the Bixby Center says parental involvement laws jeopardize the life and health of pregnant teenagers.

The Bixby Center for Global Reproductive Health is a pro-choice organization that works to provide additional choices in contraception, abortion, maternal health, and sexually transmitted infection (STI) prevention for diverse populations.

The material in the following viewpoint has been excerpted from its original version.

"Adolescents & Parental Notification for Abortion: What Can California Learn from the Experience of Other States?" *Bixby Center for Global Reproductive Health*, September 2008. Reproduced by permission.

Consider the following questions:

1. What percent of pregnant teens does the author say tell at least one parent of their decision to have an abortion without being forced to by law? What percent of fourteen-year-olds?
2. What was the effect of Mississippi's parental consent law, according to the author?
3. What percent of pregnant teens involve their parents in their decision in Minnesota, a state *with* a notification law? What percent of pregnant teens involve their parents in their decision in Wisconsin, a state *without* such a law?

The U.S. pregnancy rate for 15 to 17 year olds declined over 40% between 1990 and 2004, from 77 to 42 per 1,000 women. The birth rate declined as well: from 38 to 22 per 1,000 women aged 15 to 17 between 1990 and 2004. . . .

Despite this tremendous progress, 1 in 5 sexually active adolescents aged 15 to 17 in the US experiences an unintended pregnancy annually. In California, unintended pregnancies result in approximately 19,000 births, 16,000 abortions, and 7,000 miscarriages among 15 to 17 year olds each year. . . .

Pregnant Teens Should Not Be Forced to Talk to Their Parents

Parental communication on issues related to sex is strong without mandates.

- Over 70% of young women in the US report discussing topics related to sex with their parents.
- In California, the vast majority (79%) of young women aged 14 to 17 reports that their parents are aware of their sexual activities.

Most young women communicate with their parents about their decision to have an abortion.

- In a study of states without parental involvement laws, a majority (61%) of young women under age 18 reported that at least one parent was aware of their decision to seek abortion care. Parental involvement was even higher among younger adolescents; over 90% of 14 year olds and 74% of 15 year olds reported having at least one parent involved in their decision.

A minority of young women choose not to involve their parents in their abortion decision, and they have valid concerns for doing so.

- In states without parental involvement laws, over 30% of young women who chose not to involve their parents cited fear of physical harm, being kicked out of the house, or other abuse as part of their reason not to tell their parents. Many others report that they choose not to involve their parents because of a difficult family situation, including drug dependency, loss of jobs, health problems, and marital strain.

Laws That Limit Teens' Access to Healthcare

Thirty-five states currently enforce parental consent or notification laws. *There is tremendous variation in laws by state.* . . . The recent increase in parental involvement legislation has come in concert with other forms of legislation designed to limit adolescents' access to safe and confidential reproductive healthcare. Recent studies suggest that this trend will negatively impact the health of adolescents. In one study, adolescents reported that they will discontinue using most reproductive health services if confidentiality is not guaranteed; however, they would not refrain from having sex. Additional research has demonstrated that when teens fear that confidentiality is not

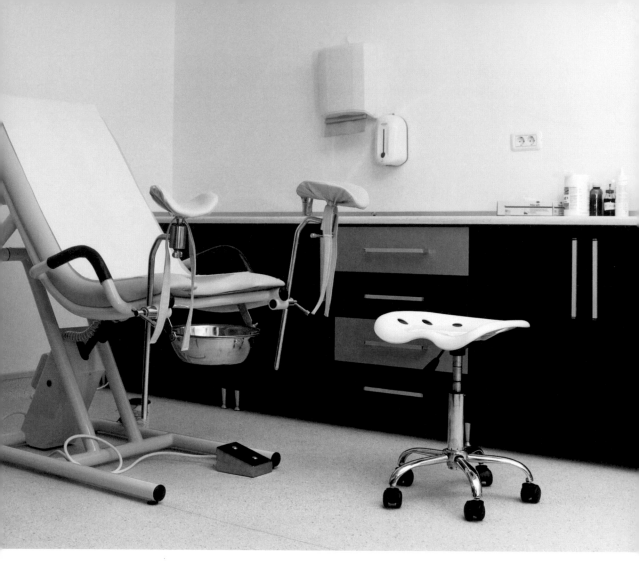

Studies suggest that enforced parental consent for teen abortions may cause teens to discontinue reproductive health services but continue to have sex.

guaranteed, they are less likely to disclose all pertinent medical history to their medical provider and are less likely to return for necessary follow-up visits.

Recognizing the importance of maintaining adolescents' confidentiality in the healthcare setting while encouraging voluntary family communication, the American Academy of Pediatrics, along with other leading public health and medical professional organizations, has issued the following policy statement:

> Adolescents should be encouraged to involve their parents and other trusted adults in reproductive

health care decisions, but this should not be mandated through parental consent or notification laws. The potential risks to adolescents if they are unable to obtain reproductive health services are so compelling that legal barriers and deference to parental involvement should not stand in the way of needed health care for patients who request confidentiality.

Obstacles to Abortion Make It More Dangerous

Parental notification and consent laws delay minors' abortions. Induced abortion is one of the safest medical procedures for women in the U.S.; however, the risk of complications increases if an abortion is delayed into the 2nd trimester. Adolescent women are most likely to experience such delays, as they take an average of one week long to identify a pregnancy and two weeks longer to seek abortion care than adult women.

Parental involvement laws increase the likelihood of delay even further. For example, adolescents who obtained an abortion after Mississippi's parental consent requirements took effect were 10–20% more likely to do so in the second trimester. The odds of a 2nd trimester abortion increased significantly for young women aged 17.5 and older after implementation of Texas' parental notification law, indicating that these women delayed their abortion care well into the 2nd trimester as a consequence of parental notification requirements.

> ### Parental Involvement Laws Put Pregnant Teens at Risk
>
> Parental notification laws cause pregnant youth to delay counseling and medical care, which can result in late-term, high-risk abortions. Some teens seek illegal, unsafe abortions or attempt suicide in order to avoid parental involvement.
>
> Asian Communities for Reproductive Justice, "No on Prop 4 Toolkit," 2008. www.reproductivejustice .org/ACRJ_No_on_Prop4_Adult_Toolkit.pdf.

Mandated parental notification does not increase parental involvement in adolescents' abortion decisions. A comparison of adolescents visiting abortion clinics in states with (Minnesota) and without (Wisconsin) notification requirements demonstrates that adolescents involve their parents in their decision at similar rates (65% and 62%, respectively). There is no evidence that a government mandate will positively increase the frequency or quality of communication for adolescents and their families.

Teens Will Find Ways Around the Law

A recent study in California surveyed young women aged 12 to 17 attending family planning clinics, asking what their response would be to a parental involvement law. Among those that would consider abortion if they became pregnant in the next 6 months, a significant proportion reported that they would plan to leave the state (37%) or country (12%) to obtain abortion care as one potential response to parental notification requirements. Additionally, 28% said that they would seek judicial bypass, and 34% said that they would "find a way around the law."

Judicial Bypass Is Not Realistic

Rather than encourage family communication, parental notification and consent laws could increase utilization of a judicial bypass option for adolescents who cannot involve their parents. Young women can bypass parental involvement requirements by going before a judge. If the judge determines that parental involvement is not in the best interest of the minor or that the minor is mature enough to make the decision on her own, the parental involvement requirement can be waived. In 2008, 540 adolescents in Massachusetts obtained a judicial bypass in order to obtain abortion care, representing nearly 10% of all adolescents having abortions in the state that year.

The court system may be unprepared to handle judicial bypass requests from adolescents, placing the adolescent at increased risk of a delayed and potentially riskier abortion. A study of Pennsylvania's

Parental Involvement Laws in America

Thirty-five states have laws that require parents to be notified or give permission in order for a pregnant teen to get an abortion. Some think these laws are unnecessary or even threaten the safety of a pregnant teen.

State	Required Parental Involvement		
	Consent Only	Notification and Consent	Notification Only
Alabama	X		
Alaska	▲		
Arizona	X		
Arkansas	X		
California	▲		
Colorado			X
Delaware			X
Florida			X
Georgia			X
Idaho	X		
Illinois			X
Indiana	X		
Iowa			X
Kansas			X
Kentucky	X		
Louisiana	X		
Massachusetts	X		
Michigan	X		
Minnesota			Both Parents
Mississippi	Both Parents		
Missouri	X		
Montana			▲
Nebraska			X
Nevada			▲
New Jersey			▲
New Mexico	▲		
North Carolina	X		
North Dakota	Both Parents		
Ohio	X		
Oklahoma		X	
Pennsylvania	X		
Rhode Island	X		
South Carolina	X		
South Dakota			X
Tennessee	X		
Texas	X		
Utah		X	
Virginia	X		
West Virginia			X
Wisconsin	X		
Wyoming	X		
TOTAL	22	2	11

Note: Except where indicated, policies require the involvement of one parent.

▲ Enforcement permanently enjoined by court order; policy not in effect.

juvenile court system demonstrated that only 8 of 60 judicial court districts provided complete information to young women inquiring about the judicial bypass option. Additionally, a young woman's access to accurate information about the bypass option was largely subject to the knowledge and willingness of individuals in her local court to disclose the information.

Increasing Runaways

The passage of parental notification and consent laws has been shown to increase the frequency with which adolescents travel out-of-state for abortion care. Incomplete data on travel and out-of-state abortion rates make it difficult to quantify the complete impact of travel on abortion rates; nonetheless, it is estimated that:

- In the 20 months following implementation of Massachusetts' parental consent law, half as many minors obtained an abortion as had done so prior to the law's implementation. During this same time period, more than 1800 minors (88% of the decrease in abortions) traveled to 5 neighboring states to have an abortion.
- In Mississippi, the abortion rate among minors did not significantly decline (<3%) after the state's parental consent law was implemented. Abortions occurring both in-state and out-of-state were included in the rate.
- After Missouri implemented its parental notification law, the in-state abortion rate for women under age 18 fell by 20%. During the same time period, the likelihood that a woman in this age group traveled out of state to obtain abortion care increased by 52%. . . .

Parental involvement laws have not been shown to change the age dynamics of relationships. Three-quarters of young women in the US choose sexual partners who are within three years of their own age. There is no evidence to support the claim that parental involvement laws will change the age dynamics of relationships or identify increased cases of sexual abuse. For example, after implementation of parental involvement laws in Texas and Arizona, the proportion of births to teen mothers involving significantly older fathers did not change.

Passing state-by-state parental consent laws may force teens to run away from their homes and have an abortion performed in another state that does not require parental consent.

Parental Involvement Laws Are Not Needed to Reduce Teen Pregnancy

Over the past decade, California has been at the forefront of successful efforts to reduce teen pregnancy and abortion rates. The state supports comprehensive family life education including key messages about both abstinence and contraception, and ensures the provision of contraceptive services for teens in a confidential manner. Adolescents in California are reporting delayed sexual activity and increases in contraceptive use. As a result, fewer adolescents experience unintended pregnancy and abortion each year. As evidenced by research from other states, requiring parental notification will likely not prevent abortion or the need for abortion, nor will it improve minors' communication with parents about abortion decisions. This research also suggests that parental notification can have the negative consequence of putting adolescents' health at risk by delaying and otherwise complicating access to care.

Analyze the essay:
1. Think about the teenagers you know. Imagine that one of them got pregnant. How do you think a parental involvement law might help this person? How might such a law hurt her?
2. Both the Bixby Center and the National Right to Life Educational Fund (the author of the previous essay) claim to have pregnant teens' best interests at heart. Yet they have very different opinions on whether parental involvement laws help or hurt such teens. After reading both essays, do you think parental involvement laws protect or hurt pregnant teens? What pieces of evidence convinced you?

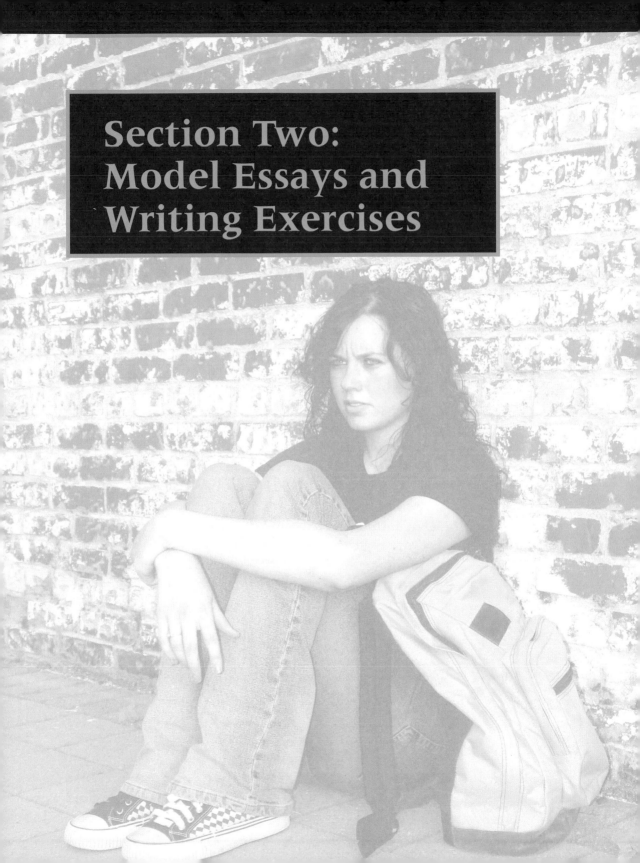

Section Two:
Model Essays and
Writing Exercises

The Five-Paragraph Essay

An *essay* is a short piece of writing that discusses or analyzes one topic. The five-paragraph essay is a form commonly used in school assignments and tests. Every five-paragraph essay begins with an *introduction*, ends with a *conclusion*, and features three *supporting paragraphs* in the middle.

The Thesis Statement. The introduction includes the essay's thesis statement. The thesis statement presents the argument or point the author is trying to make about the topic. The essays in this book all have different thesis statements because they are making different arguments about teen pregnancy.

The thesis statement should clearly tell the reader what the essay will be about. A focused thesis statement helps determine what will be in the essay; the subsequent paragraphs are spent developing and supporting its argument.

The Introduction. In addition to presenting the thesis statement, a well-written introductory paragraph captures the attention of the reader and explains why the topic being explored is important. It may provide the reader with background information on the subject matter or feature an anecdote that illustrates a point relevant to the topic. It could also present startling information that clarifies the point of the essay or put forth a contradictory position that the essay will refute. Further techniques for writing an introduction are found later in this section.

The Supporting Paragraphs. The introduction is followed by three (or more) supporting paragraphs. These are the main body of the essay. Each paragraph presents and develops a *subtopic* that supports the essay's thesis statement. Each subtopic is spearheaded by a *topic sentence* and supported by its own facts, details, and examples. The writer can use various kinds of supporting material and details to back up the topic of each supporting paragraph. These may include statistics, quotations from people with special knowledge or expertise, historic facts, and anecdotes. A rule of writing is that specific and concrete examples are more convincing than vague, general, or unsupported assertions.

The Conclusion. The conclusion is the paragraph that closes the essay. Its function is to summarize or reiterate the main idea of the essay. It may recall an idea from the introduction or briefly examine the larger implications of the thesis. Because the conclusion is also the last chance a writer has to make an impression on the reader, it is important that it not simply repeat what has been presented elsewhere in the essay but close it in a clear, final, and memorable way.

Although the order of the essay's component paragraphs is important, they do not have to be written in the order presented here. Some writers like to decide on a thesis and write the introduction paragraph first. Other writers like to focus first on the body of the essay and write the introduction and conclusion later.

Pitfalls to Avoid

When writing essays about controversial issues such as teen pregnancy, it is important to remember that disputes over the material are common precisely because there are many different perspectives. Remember to state your arguments in careful and measured terms. Evaluate your topic fairly—avoid overstating negative qualities of one perspective or understating positive qualities of another. Use examples, facts, and details to support any assertions you make.

The Persuasive Essay

There are many types of essays, but in general, they are usually short compositions in which the writer expresses and discusses an opinion about something. In the persuasive essay the writer tries to persuade (convince) the reader to do something or to agree with the writer's opinion about something. Examples of persuasive writing are easy to find. Advertising is one common example. Through commercial and print ads, companies try to convince the public to buy their products for specific reasons. A lot of everyday writing is persuasive, too. Letters to the editor, posts from sports fans on team Web sites, even handwritten notes urging a friend to listen to a new CD—all are examples of persuasive writing.

The Tools of Persuasion

The writer of the persuasive essay uses various tools to persuade the reader. Here are some of them:

Facts and Statistics. A fact is a statement that no one, typically, would disagree with. It can be verified by information in reputable resources, such as encyclopedias, almanacs, government Web sites, or reference books about the topic of the fact.

Examples of Facts and Statistics

Independence Day is celebrated on July 4.

Albany is the capital of New York.

Fewer than 1 percent of pregnant teens give their babies up for adoption.

According to a July 2009 Gallup poll, 61 percent of Americans believe it was a mistake to have gone to war in Afghanistan.

It is important to note that facts and statistics can be *misstated* (written down or quoted incorrectly), *misinterpreted* (not understood correctly by the user), or *misused* (not used fairly). But, if a writer uses facts and statistics properly, they can add authority to the writer's essay.

Opinions. An opinion is what a person thinks about something. It can be contested or argued with. However, opinions of people who are experts on the topic or who have personal experience are often very convincing. Many persuasive essays are written to convince the reader that the writer's opinion is worth believing and acting on.

Testimonials. A testimonial is a statement given by a person who is thought to be an expert or who has another trait people admire, such as being a celebrity. Television commercials frequently use testimonials to convince watchers to buy the products they are advertising.

Examples. An example is something that is representative of a group or type ("Labrador retriever" is an example of the group "dog"). Examples are used to help define, describe, or illustrate something to make it more understandable.

Anecdotes. Anecdotes are extended examples. They are little stories with a beginning, middle, and end. They can be used just like examples to explain something or to show something about a topic.

Appeals to Reason. One way to convince readers that an opinion or action is right is to appeal to reason or logic. This often involves the idea that if some ideas are true, another must also be true. Here is an example of one type of appeal to reason:

— Eating fast food causes obesity and diabetes, just as smoking cigarettes causes lung cancer and asthma. For this reason, fast food companies, like cigarette manufacturers, should be held legally responsible for their customers' health.

Appeals to Emotion. Another way to persuade readers to believe or do something is to appeal to their emotions— love, fear, pity, loyalty, and anger are some of the emotions to which writers appeal. A writer who wants to persuade someone not to eat meat might appeal to their love of animals:

— If you own a cat, dog, hamster, or bird, you should not eat meat. It makes no sense to pamper and love your pet while at the same time supporting the merciless slaughter of other animals for your dinner.

Ridicule and Name-Calling. Ridicule and name-calling are not good techniques to use in a persuasive essay. Instead of exploring the strengths of the topic, the writer who uses these relies on making those who oppose the main idea look foolish, evil, or stupid. In most cases, the writer who does this weakens the argument.

Bandwagon. The writer who uses the bandwagon technique uses the idea that "Everybody thinks this or is doing this; therefore it is valid." The bandwagon method is not a very authoritative way to convince your reader of your point.

Words and Phrases Common to Persuasive Essays

accordingly	it stands to reason
because	it then follows that
clearly	obviously
consequently	since
for this reason	subsequently
indeed	therefore
it is necessary to	this is why
it makes sense to	thus
it seems clear that	we must

Poverty Causes Teen Pregnancy

Essay
One

Editor's Notes Persuasive essays commonly attempt to persuade a reader to agree that there is a specific reason or cause for a problem. This is the goal of the following model essay. It argues that teen pregnancy is caused by poverty. The author offers three reasons why it is reasonable to think that poverty contributes to teen pregnancy. The essay is structured as a five-paragraph essay in which each paragraph contributes a supporting piece of evidence to develop the argument.

The notes in the margin point out key features of the essay and will help you understand how the essay is organized. Also note that all sources are cited using Modern Language Association (MLA) style.* For more information on how to cite your sources see Appendix C. In addition, consider the following:

1. How does the introduction engage the reader's attention?
2. What persuasive techniques are used in the essay?
3. What purpose do the essay's quotes serve?
4. Does the essay convince you of its point?

Refers to thesis and topic sentences

Refers to supporting details

Paragraph 1

Teen pregnancy is an ongoing problem in the United States and one that is even on the rise. In their desperation to curb the problem, health officials, sociologists, and policy experts tend to focus on two main culprits: abstinence-only education or comprehensive sex education. One camp says teaching young people only to abstain from sex fails

Look at Exercise 3A on introductions. What type of introduction is this? Does it grab your attention?

---

* Editor's Note: In applying MLA style guidelines in this book, the following simplifications have been made: Parenthetical text citations are confined to direct quotations only; electronic source documentation in the Works Cited list omits date of access, page ranges, and some detailed facts of publication.

to give them the tools they need to prevent pregnancy; the other accuses comprehensive sex education programs of encouraging kids to have sex too early. But it is likely that both camps are entirely wrong: A bigger factor than what kind of sex education a teen receives may be her socioeconomic status. Poverty, not sex education or lack thereof, is the chief cause of teen pregnancy in the United States.

This is the essay's thesis statement. It tells the reader what will be argued in the following paragraphs.

Paragraph 2

The poverty–teen pregnancy connection works like this: Teenagers who get pregnant are more likely to drop out of school, which in turn sentences them to low-paying jobs. Teen mothers are also less likely to get married, which means they must struggle to raise a child on one income. According to Sarah S. Brown of the National Campaign to Prevent Teen Pregnancy, these factors make teenage mothers unlikely to find "a way out from what is often a low-income community to begin with" (qtd. in Connolly A10). According to figures published in the *San Francisco Chronicle*, about two-thirds of teenage mothers live at or below the poverty line. Says Jonathan Zimmerman, a professor of history and education at New York University, "Americans have it exactly backward. Teen pregnancy doesn't deprive our kids of life chances; instead, kids who lack those chances are the ones who get pregnant" (B7).

This is the topic sentence of Paragraph 2. It is a subset of the essay's thesis. It tells what specific point this paragraph will be about.

Note how these quotes support the ideas discussed in the paragraph. They also come from reputable sources.

Paragraph 3

Zimmerman and others speculate that one reason poor teens get pregnant is because they lack confidence, which is possessed in greater amounts by higher-income girls. He has suggested that impoverished girls lack the confidence to demand their partners use protection—teens from higher-income families, however, have a heightened sense of power and confidence and thus are better at removing themselves from situations that might lead to pregnancy, such as unprotected sex, sex too early, or nonconsensual sex. "Impoverished girls often lack that confidence, so they don't take measures to protect themselves" (Zimmerman B7). Poor teens may also be lacking love and support from

This is the topic sentence of Paragraph 3. Without reading the rest of the paragraph, take a guess at what the paragraph will be about.

What point in Paragraph 3 does this quote support?

their families and may be fooled into thinking that having a baby offers them someone who will love them unconditionally and whom they can love back.

Paragraph 4

Poverty seems to be a likely cause of teen pregnancy when one considers that both abstinence-only and comprehensive sex education programs have met with mixed success and failure. Neither approach can point to total success. For example, some studies have shown abstinence-only programs to be effective at delaying teenage sex, while others reveal that when such teens finally do have sex, they are less likely to use protection. Comprehensive sex education, on the other hand, is often derided for sending teens mixed messages about their bodies and also for touting condoms as foolproof—when in fact, many condoms break or slip. Refocusing the debate on poverty and how it contributes to teen pregnancy could do more to help. As Brown says, "People love to argue about how to prevent teen pregnancy, but sometimes we fail to shine enough light on the basic problem" (qtd. in Connolly A10).

How is the topic of Paragraph 4 different, but related, to the other topics discussed thus far?

"For example" and "on the other hand" are transitional phrases. They keep the sentences linked and the ideas moving.

Paragraph 5

Experts seeking to prevent teen pregnancy would do well to stop quibbling about sex education approaches and focus more on the link between poverty and teen pregnancy. Doing so could prevent the births of hundreds of thousands of unwanted babies and the ruined lives of their teenage parents. As Zimmerman warns, "The more we fight about teen pregnancy, the less we'll focus upon teen poverty. And that's bad news for all of us" (B7).

This sentence serves to wrap up what the essay has discussed. It does so without repeating every point that was made.

Works Cited

Connolly, Ceci. "As Teen Pregnancy Dropped, So Did Child Poverty." *Washington Post* 14 Apr 2005: A10.

Zimmerman, Jonathan. "Poverty, Not Sex Ed, Key Factor in Teen Pregnancy." *San Francisco Chronicle* 4 Sept 2008: B7.

Exercise 1A: Create an Outline from an Existing Essay

It often helps to create an outline of the five-paragraph essay before you write it. The outline can help you organize the information, arguments, and evidence you have gathered during your research.

For this exercise, create an outline that could have been used to write "Poverty Causes Teen Pregnancy." This "reverse engineering" exercise is meant to help familiarize you with how outlines can help classify and arrange information.

To do this you will need to
1. articulate the essay's thesis,
2. pinpoint important pieces of evidence,
3. flag quotes that supported the essay's ideas, and
4. identify key points that supported the argument.

Part of the outline has already been started to give you an idea of the assignment.

Outline
I. Paragraph 1
Write the essay's thesis:

II. Paragraph 2
Topic:

Supporting Detail i. Two-thirds of teenage mothers live at or below the poverty line.
Supporting Detail ii.

III. Paragraph 3
Topic: One reason poor teen girls get pregnant is because they lack confidence.

Supporting Detail i.

Supporting Detail ii. Quote from Jonathan Zimmerman supporting the argument that poor teen girls get pregnant because they lack confidence.

IV. Paragraph 4
Topic:

Supporting Detail i. Ways in which both abstinence-only and comprehensive sex education programs have failed to adequately prevent teen pregnancy.
Supporting Detail ii.

V. Paragraph 5:
Write the essay's conclusion:

Exercise 1B: Create an Outline for Your Own Essay

The model essay you just read expresses a particular point of view about teen pregnancy. For this exercise, your assignment is to find supporting ideas, choose specific and concrete details, create an outline, and ultimately write a five-paragraph essay making a different, or even opposing, point about teen pregnancy. Your goal is to use persuasive techniques to convince your reader.

Part 1: Write a thesis statement.
The following thesis statement would be appropriate for an opposing essay on why comprehensive sex education programs cause teen pregnancy:

When we teach young people about birth control based on the assumption that "they are going to have sex anyway," we essentially sentence them to live up to our expectations.

Or see the sample paper topics suggested in Appendix D for more ideas.

Part II: Brainstorm pieces of supporting evidence.

Using information from some of the viewpoints in the previous section and from the information found in Section Three of this book, write down three arguments or pieces of evidence that support the thesis statement you selected. Then, for each of these three arguments, write down facts, examples, and details that support it. These could be

- statistical information
- personal memories and anecdotes
- quotes from experts, peers, or family members
- observations of people's actions and behaviors
- specific and concrete details

Supporting pieces of evidence for the above sample thesis statement are found in this book and include:

- Studies reported in Viewpoint Two by Katherine Bradley and Christine Kim showing that abstinence programs reduce and delay teen sex.
- Chart accompanying Viewpoint Two that shows that the majority of parents support abstinence-based education programs.
- Quote accompanying Viewpoint Two by social psychologist Stan Weed, who testified on the issue before the House of Representatives: "Emerging evidence supports the notion that abstinence-centered

strategies, if well-designed and implemented, can significantly and substantially reduce teen sexual initiation for periods of 1 to 2 years and thereby may positively impact the health of American adolescents." The full link to Weed's testimony is http://oversight.house.gov/documents/20080423114651.pdf. More information that can support this topic is found here.

Part III: Place the information from Part I in outline form.

Part IV: Write the arguments or supporting statements in paragraph form.

By now you have three arguments that support the paragraph's thesis statement, as well as supporting material. Use the outline to write out your three supporting arguments in paragraph form. Make sure each paragraph has a topic sentence that states the paragraph's thesis clearly and broadly. Then, add supporting sentences that express the facts, quotes, details, and examples that support the paragraph's argument. The paragraph may also have a concluding or summary sentence.

Christian Conservatives Are to Blame for the Rise in Teen Pregnancy

Editor's Notes The following model essay argues that Christian conservatives are to blame for the rise in teen pregnancy. Like the first model essay, this essay is structured as a five-paragraph persuasive essay in which each paragraph contributes a supporting piece of evidence to develop the argument. Each supporting paragraph explores one of three distinct reasons that the author thinks conservative religious thinking has helped increase teen pregnancy.

As you read this essay, take note of its components and how they are organized (the notes in the margins provide further explanation).

Paragraph 1

What is the essay's thesis statement? How did you recognize it?

After years of decline, teen pregnancy is once again on the rise in the United States. According to the National Center for Health Statistics, the teen birth rate in the United States rose 3.5 percent in 2006 after enjoying a fourteen-year decline and rose again in 2007. In fact, the number of teen births has not been this high since 1989. The cause? The influx of conservative Christian thinking promoted under the administration of former president George W. Bush.

Paragraph 2

This is the topic sentence of Paragraph 2. Note that all of the paragraph's details fit with it—or *support* it.

The seeds for this problem were sown in the early years of the Bush administration, which promoted and heavily funded conservative abstinence-only education programs. Throughout the 1990s, under the presidency of Democrat Bill Clinton, teen pregnancy declined. In fact, between 1990 and 2004 the birth rate among teenage girls fell a sharp and impressive 46 percent. A study published by the *American Journal of Public Health* attributed 86 percent of the decline during these years to better use of contraceptives. But halfway through Bush's presidency, the decline in teen pregnancy began to reverse itself. By 2006, teen births had increased for the first time since 1991. So teaching about condoms helped reduce the teen birth rate—until George W. Bush and his conservative zealot friends came along.

> Identify a piece of evidence used to support Paragraph 2's main idea.

Paragraph 3

Put simply, more teens became pregnant because they did not get enough information about birth control. This is confirmed by a survey undertaken by the Department of Health and Human Services, which found that while more than 80 percent of teenagers received abstinence instruction, fewer than 70 percent received information about birth control. This is the problem with the abstinence-only education programs that Christian conservatives favor—in encouraging teens to abstain, they rob them of the information and tools needed to protect themselves when they do have sex. In fact, a study published in the *Journal of Adolescent Health* found that 88 percent of teens who take virginity pledges—religious-based promises to remain virgins until marriage—end up breaking their pledge while they are still in their teenage years. When they do have sex, they are less likely to use condoms—and thus more likely to end up pregnant. The best way to avoid pregnancy is to use condoms, but sadly, America's teens have not been taught this.

> This is the topic sentence of Paragraph 3. Without reading the rest of the paragraph, take a guess at what the paragraph will be about.

> "In fact" is a transitional phrase that helps keep the ideas in the essay flowing. Make a list of all transitional words and phrases used in the essay.

> This is a *supporting detail*. This information directly supports the topic sentence, helping to prove it true.

Paragraph 4

Because Christian conservativism is to blame for the increase in teen births, readers will not be surprised to learn that nine of the ten states with the highest increase in teenage births voted Republican in the 2000 and 2004 presidential elections, and eight voted Republican in the 2008 election. Among them are Alabama, Kentucky, Louisiana, Mississippi, and Oklahoma, all Bible-Belt heartland states. These are the states in which Bush's

> What is the main point of Paragraph 4? How is it related to the essay's thesis?

abstinence campaigns were most enthusiastically promoted and the places in which conservatives most loudly thump their fists and call for increases in abstinence-only education programs, even as their own children are getting pregnant. It is in these states where "the conservatives have gone ballistic," says columnist George Monbiot, who thinks abstinence-only programs are worse than useless. "They still insist that American children should be deprived of sex education, lied to about contraception and maintained in a state of medieval ignorance. If their own children end up with syphilis or unwanted babies, that, it seems, is a price they will pay for preserving their beliefs."

The author quotes a writer who makes a particularly impassioned and memorable statement about this issue. The quote matches the author's main argument.

Paragraph 5

The bottom line is that kids need sex education and access to contraception if they are to avoid getting pregnant. Teens are going to have sex, so they might as well be armed with the right information and tools so they can best protect themselves from the experience. Christian conservatives seem to wishfully think that simply forbidding teen sexuality can prevent teen pregnancy. The rise in the teen birth rate under their watch should be all the evidence to the contrary that is needed.

After reading the essay, are you convinced of the author's point? If so, what evidence swayed you? If not, why not?

Works Cited

Monbiot, George. "These Denialogues Don't Care If Their Own Children End Up with Syphilis." *Guardian* (Manchester, UK) 27 Jul 2009.

Exercise 2A: Create an Outline from an Existing Essay

As you did for the first model essay in this section, create an outline that could have been used to write "Christian Conservatives Are to Blame for the Rise in Teen Pregnancy." Be sure to identify the essay's thesis statement, its supporting ideas and details, and key pieces of evidence that were used.

Exercise 2B: Identify Persuasive Techniques

Essayists use many techniques to get you to agree with their ideas or to do something they want you to do. Some of the most common techniques are described in Preface B of this section, "The Persuasive Essay." These tools are facts and statistics, opinions, testimonials, examples and anecdotes, appeals to reason, appeals to emotion, ridicule and name-calling, and bandwagon. Go back to the preface and review these tools. Remember that most of these tools can be used to enhance your essay, but some of them—particularly ridiculing, name-calling, and bandwagon—can detract from the essay's effectiveness. Nevertheless, you should be able to recognize them in the essays you read.

Some writers use one persuasive tool throughout their whole essay. For example, the essay may be one extended anecdote, or the writer may rely entirely on statistics. But most writers typically use a combination of persuasive tools. Model Essay Two, "Christian Conservatives Are to Blame for the Rise in Teen Pregnancy," does this.

Problem One
Read Model Essay Two again and see if you can find every persuasive tool used. Put that information in the following table. Part of the table is filled in for you.

Explanatory notes are underneath the table. (Note: You will not fill in every box. No paragraph contains all of the techniques.)

	Paragraph 1 Sentence #	Paragraph 2 Sentence #	Paragraph 3 Sentence #	Paragraph 4 Sentence #	Paragraph 5 Sentence #
Fact				1[e]	
Statistic	2[a]		2[c]		
Opinion			6[d]		
Testimonial					
Example					
Anecdote					
Appeal to Reason		8[c]			
Appeal to Emotion					
Ridicule		7[b]			
Name-Calling					
Bandwagon					

Notes

a. That the teen birth rate in the United States rose 3.5 percent in 2006 after enjoying a fourteen-year decline is a *statistic*.
b. When the author refers to "George W. Bush and his conservative zealot friends," she is *ridiculing* them.
c. The findings of the Department of Health and Human Services are *statistics*.
d. It is the author's *opinion* that the best way to avoid pregnancy is to use condoms.
e. It is a *fact* that nine of the ten states with the highest increase in teenage births voted Republican in the 2000 and 2004 presidential elections, and eight voted Republican in the 2008 election.

Now, look at the table you have produced. Which persuasive tools does this essay rely on most heavily? Which are not used at all?

Problem Two
Apply this exercise to the other model essays in this section and the viewpoints in Section One, when you are finished reading them.

Why Parental Involvement Laws Are Always Wrong

Editor's Notes The final model essay argues that pregnant teens should not have to notify their parents or get their permission to get birth control, emergency contraception, or have an abortion. Supported by facts, quotes, statistics and opinions, it tries to persuade the reader that the existence of parental involvement laws poses a threat to pregnant teens by making them less likely to seek medical care at a time when they need it most.

This essay differs from the previous model essays in that it is longer than five paragraphs. Sometimes five paragraphs are simply not enough to adequately develop an idea. Extending the length of an essay can allow the reader to explore a topic in more depth or present multiple pieces of evidence that together provide a complete picture of a topic. Longer essays can also help readers discover the complexity of a subject by examining a topic beyond its superficial exterior. Moreover, the ability to write a sustained research or position paper is a valuable skill you will need as you advance academically.

As you read, consider the questions posed in the margins. Continue to identify thesis statements, supporting details, transitions, and quotations. Examine the introductory and concluding paragraphs to understand how they give shape to the essay. Finally, evaluate the essay's general structure and assess its overall effectiveness.

Refers to thesis and topic sentences

Refers to supporting details

Paragraph 1

A majority of Americans strongly support laws that require a pregnant teenager to either alert or get the permission of a parent before she has an abortion (otherwise known as parental notification or parental consent laws). This is why they have been adopted by thirty-five states. But such laws are the wrong approach to preventing teen pregnancy or curbing teen abortion. Instead, they jeopardize the health and safety of pregnant teens and have little or no effect on teen pregnancy rates or teen abortion rates. For this reason, consent or notification should never be required for minors seeking an abortion, and states with such laws should abandon them immediately.

What is the essay's thesis statement? How did you recognize it?

Paragraph 2

One reason that parental involvement laws are unnecessary is that pregnant teens are already talking to their parents about their problem without being forced to by law. According to the California Adolescent Health Collaborative (AHC), more than 60 percent of teens naturally turn to their parents when they find out they are pregnant. More than 90 percent of teens fourteen and under naturally turn to their parents when they become pregnant. In other words, the majority of teens will invite their parents into their lives when facing this overwhelming problem.

Paragraph 3

Proving that parental involvement laws are ineffective is the fact that pregnant teens who live in states without involvement laws turn to their parents at the same rate as teens in states with them. For example, according to the Bixby Center for Global Reproductive Health, 65 percent of pregnant teens in Minnesota—a state with a parental notification law—talk to their parents about their unplanned pregnancy. Meanwhile, 62 percent of pregnant teens in Wisconsin—a state without a parental notification law—talk to their parents about their unplanned pregnancy. This shows that teens are talking to their parents about this intimate and pressing problem at about the same rate regardless of whether the law forces them to. Furthermore, when pregnant teens feel unable to consult with their parents, data from states without parental involvement laws show

This information was taken from Viewpoint 6. This book contains many resources for writing an essay on teen pregnancy.

that almost all talk to another close relative, such as a grandparent or aunt. The end result? Teens are talking to the people who care about them regardless of what the law says.

Paragraph 4

As for those teenagers who do not talk to their parents, it is suspected that they have very good reason to avoid the conversation. In fact, about 33 percent of pregnant teens say they cannot talk to their parents about their pregnancy because they have been abused by at least one parent in the past and fear their parents will react violently if they find out about their pregnancy. Common fears include being beaten, being kicked out of the house, or facing another form of abuse.

Paragraph 5

In rare cases, some teens become pregnant as a result of incest. In this case, forcing them to tell their abuser about their decision to seek an abortion can be especially dangerous. It is feared that abusers will hurt or even kill the pregnant girl to prevent health care providers from finding out how the baby was conceived. This is what happened to a thirteen-year-old girl from Idaho named Spring Adams. Spring was shot to death by her father after he found out she planned to seek an abortion for a pregnancy he caused. Spring was one of the girls "who do not involve a parent [because they] come from families where government-mandated disclosure would have dev-astating effects" (NARAL Pro-Choice America, 2). Spring is one of the many examples of the way in which laws that force communication between parents and pregnant teens can further hurt young people who are already in danger.

Identify a piece of evidence used to support Paragraph 5's main idea.

Paragraph 6

Parental involvement laws might also end up encouraging pregnant teens to hurt themselves. If a teenager is being forced by the state to get parental consent for an abortion, and she feels she cannot talk to her parents, she will likely end up trying to force an abortion on her own. This may cost her her life. The most famous example of such a tragedy is Becky Bell, a teenage girl from Indianapolis who died after receiving a back-alley, or illegal, abortion in 1988. Bell received the illegal abortion because in order to receive a legal one, she would have had to tell her parents. But Becky felt she could not tell her parents about her pregnancy—she feared they would be too disappointed in her. Within a week of receiving the illegal abortion, she died from an infection. Other teens who are too scared to tell their parents about their need for a safe and legal abortion may resort to other methods, such as swallowing dangerous poisons, having someone hit them in the stomach with a baseball bat, or even putting sharp objects inside their vagina. All of these threaten a girl's health, her future fertility, and even her life.

What persuasive techniques has the author used thus far? See Preface B in this section for information on persuasive techniques.

Make a list of all the transitions that appear in the essay, and note how they keep the ideas flowing.

Paragraph 7

Parental involvement laws also endanger a pregnant teen's health by causing her to delay her decision to get an abortion. Although abortion is typically a safe procedure, abortions are safest when they are done in the first trimester. But teens who are forced to tell their parents about their pregnancy tend to push back the unpleasant discussion by weeks, even months. Not knowing how to broach the topic—or fearing the response of their parents—their decision to have an abortion is delayed, which in turn delays their abortion. The *Los Angeles Times* reports that teens are twice as likely as adults to delay pregnancy-related care anyway—most do not need the added delay of working up the nerve to involve their parents in the decision. Says columnist Miriam Gerace, "Experience from some states with notification laws shows us that teens will avoid doctors and delay getting an abortion later into a pregnancy—sometimes as late as the second trimester, when abortion is a more complicated procedure."

What is the topic sentence of Paragraph 7? What pieces of evidence are used to show it is true?

Finally, parental involvement laws should be rejected because they just do not work—most appear to have little or no effect on teen pregnancy rates, and in some cases even increase them. This was the finding of a ground-breaking analysis by the *New York Times*, which looked at parental notification and consent laws in six states over a nine-year period. It found "no evidence that the laws had a significant impact on the number of minors who got pregnant, or, once pregnant, the number who had abortion" (Lehren and Leland). In fact, in three of the states—Arizona, Idaho, and Tennessee—the percentage of pregnant minors who had abortions actually rose slightly after the consent laws went into effect. Abortion providers speculate that the laws do not work because they have little connection to most pregnant teens' realities—most pregnant teens talk to their parents about their problem anyway, and those who feel they cannot will not be forced into the conversation by law.

What experts or organizations are quoted in the essay? Make a list of every person quoted, along with his or her credentials.

Their ineffectiveness and the way they endanger teens are just a few of the reasons why several major American medical organizations oppose parental involvement laws. Among them are the American Academy of Pediatrics, the Society for Adolescent Medicine, the American Academy of Family Physicians, the California Medical Association, and the American College of Obstetricians and Gynecologists. If the nation's foremost medical providers are against forcing teens to talk to their parents about abortion, surely it is the wrong approach to curbing teen pregnancy in the United States. As the California Adolescent Health Collaborative has said, "Parental notification laws do not increase family communication as would be desirable. Instead they appear to cause delays in receiving services and cause an undue burden on all those involved."

Paragraph 10

Parental involvement laws do not work. Most pregnant teens will talk to their parents about their problem. Those who do not have a good reason to avoid the conversation, and forcing them to talk to violent parents only puts them in harm's way. For these reasons and more, such laws should be repealed in states that have adopted them. Those seeking to protect minors from the harsh realities of teen pregnancy would do well to invest in better sex education programs and other preventive strategies.

After reading the essay, are you convinced of the author's point? If so, what evidence swayed you? If not, why not?

Works Cited

California Adolescent Health Collaborative. "Involving Parents in Reproductive Health Decisions." < www .reproductivejustice.org/download/Prop85/involving_ parents.pdf > .

Gerace, Miriam. "What a Doctor Says About Adolescent Healthcare." *Los Angeles Times* 22 Oct 2008.

Lehren, Andrew, and John Leland. "Scant Drop Seen in Abortion Rate If Parents Are Told." *New York Times* 6 Mar 2006

NARAL Pro-Choice America. "Mandatory Parental- Involvement Laws Threaten Young Women's Safety." 1 Jan 2009 < www.prochoiceamerica.org/assets/ files/Abortion-Access-to-Abortion-Young-Women- Parental-Consent.pdf > .

Exercise 3A: Examining Introductions and Conclusions

Every essay features introductory and concluding paragraphs that are used to frame the main ideas being presented. Along with presenting the essay's thesis statement, well-written introductions should grab the attention of the reader and make clear why the topic being explored is important. The conclusion reiterates the essay's thesis and is also the last chance for the writer to make an impression on the reader. Strong introductions and conclusions can greatly enhance an essay's effect on an audience.

The Introduction

There are several techniques that can be used to craft an introductory paragraph. An essay can start with:

- an anecdote: a brief story that illustrates a point relevant to the topic;
- startling information: facts or statistics that elucidate the point of the essay;
- setting up and knocking down a position: a position or claim believed by proponents of one side of a controversy, followed by statements that challenge that claim;
- historical perspective: an example of the way things used to be that leads into a discussion of how or why things work differently now;
- summary information: general introductory information about the topic that feeds into the essay's thesis statement.

1. Reread the introductory paragraphs of the model essays and of the viewpoints in Section One. Identify which of the techniques described above are used in the example essays. How do they grab the attention of the reader? Are their thesis statements clearly presented?
2. Write an introduction for the essay you have outlined and partially written in Exercise 1B using one of the techniques described above.

The Conclusion

The conclusion brings the essay to a close by summarizing or returning to its main ideas. Good conclusions, however, go beyond simply repeating these ideas. Strong conclusions explore a topic's broader implications and reiterate why it is important to consider. They may frame the essay by returning to an anecdote featured in the opening paragraph. Or they may close with a quotation or refer back to an event in the essay. In opinionated essays, the conclusion can reiterate which side the essay is taking or ask the reader to reconsider a previously held position on the subject.

3. Reread the concluding paragraphs of the model essays and of the viewpoints in Section I. Which were most effective in driving their arguments home to the reader? What sorts of techniques did they use to do this? Did they appeal emotionally to the reader, or bookend an idea or event referenced elsewhere in the essay?

4. Write a conclusion for the essay you have outlined and partially written in Exercise 1B using one of the techniques described above.

Exercise 3B: Using Quotations to Enliven Your Essay

No essay is complete without quotations. Get in the habit of using quotes to support at least some of the ideas in your essays. Quotes do not need to appear in every paragraph, but often enough so that the essay contains voices aside from your own. When you write, use quotations to accomplish the following:

- Provide expert advice that you are not necessarily in me position to know about.
- Cite lively or passionate passages.
- Include a particularly well-written point that gets to the heart of the matter.
- Supply statistics or facts that have been derived from someone's research.

- Deliver anecdotes that illustrate the point you are trying to make.
- Express first-person testimony.

Problem One:

Reread the essays presented in the first two sections of this book and find at least one example of each of the above quotation types.

There are a couple of important things to remember when using quotations.

- Note your sources' qualifications and biases. This way your reader can identity the person you have quoted and can put their words in a context.
- Put any quoted material within proper quotation marks. Failing to attribute quotes to their authors constitutes plagiarism, which is when an author takes someone else's words or ideas and presents them as his of her own. Plagiarism is a very serious infraction and must be avoided at all costs.

Write Your Own Persuasive Five-Paragraph Essay

Using the information from this book, write your own five-paragraph persuasive essay that deals with teen pregnancy. You can use the resources in this book for information about issues relating to this topic and how to structure this type of essay.

The following steps are suggestions on how to get started.

Step One: Choose your topic.

The first step is to decide what topic to write your persuasive essay on. Is there anything that particularly fascinates you about teen pregnancy? Is there an aspect of the topic you strongly support, or feel strongly against? Is there an issue you feel personally connected to or one that you would like to learn more about? Ask yourself such questions before selecting your essay topic. Refer to Appendix D: Sample Essay Topics if you need help selecting a topic.

Step Two: Write down questions and answers about the topic.

Before you begin writing, you will need to think carefully about what ideas your essay will contain. This is a process known as *brainstorming*. Brainstorming involves asking yourself questions and coming up with ideas to discuss in your essay. Possible questions that will help you with the brainstorming process include:
- Why is this topic important?
- Why should people be interested in this topic?
- How can I make this essay interesting to the reader?
- What question am I going to address in this paragraph or essay?
- What facts, ideas, or quotes can I use to support the answer to my question?

Questions especially for persuasive essays include:
- Is there something I want to convince my reader of?
- Is there a topic I want to advocate in favor of, or rally against?

- Is there enough evidence to support my opinion?
- Do I want to make a call to action—motivate my readers to do something about a particular problem or event?

Step Three: Gather facts, ideas, and anecdotes related to your topic.

This book contains several places to find information about many aspects of teen pregnancy, including the viewpoints and the appendices. In addition, you may want to research the books, articles, and Web sites listed in Section Three, or do additional research in your local library. You can also conduct an interview if you know someone who has a compelling story that would fit well in your essay.

Step Four: Develop a workable, thesis statement.

Use what you have written down in steps two and three to help you articulate the main point or argument you want to make in your essay. It should be expressed in a clear sentence and make an arguable or supportable point.

Example:

Telling teens they should wait to have sex and then supplying them with condoms sends a mixed message that tragically backfires.

This could be the thesis statement of a persuasive essay that argues that abstinence-only sex education programs are the best way to prevent teen pregnancy.

Step Five: Write an outline or diagram.

1. Write the thesis statement at the top of the outline.
2. Write roman numerals I, II, and III on the left side of the page with A, B, and C under each numeral.
3. Next to each roman numeral, write down the best ideas you came up with in step three. These should all directly relate to and support the thesis statement.
4. Next to each letter write down information that supports that particular idea.

Step Six: Write the three supporting paragraphs.
Use your outline to write the three supporting paragraphs. Write down the main idea of each paragraph in sentence form. Do the same thing for the supporting points of information. Each sentence should support the paragraph of the topic. Be sure you have relevant and interesting details, facts, and quotes. Use transitions when you move from idea to idea to keep the text fluid and smooth. Sometimes, although not always, paragraphs can include a concluding or summary sentence that restates the paragraph's argument.

Step Seven: Write the introduction and conclusion.
See Exercise 3A for information on writing introductions and conclusions.

Step Eight: Read and rewrite.
As you read, check your essay for the following:

- ✔ Does the essay maintain a consistent tone?
- ✔ Do all paragraphs reinforce your general thesis?
- ✔ Do all paragraphs flow from one to the other? Do you need to add transition words or phrases?
- ✔ Have you quoted from reliable, authoritative, and interesting sources?
- ✔ Is there a sense of progression throughout the essay?
- ✔ Does the essay get bogged down in too much detail or irrelevant material?
- ✔ Does your introduction grab the reader's attention?
- ✔ Does your conclusion reflect on any previously discussed material, or give the essay a sense of closure?
- ✔ Are there any spelling or grammatical errors?

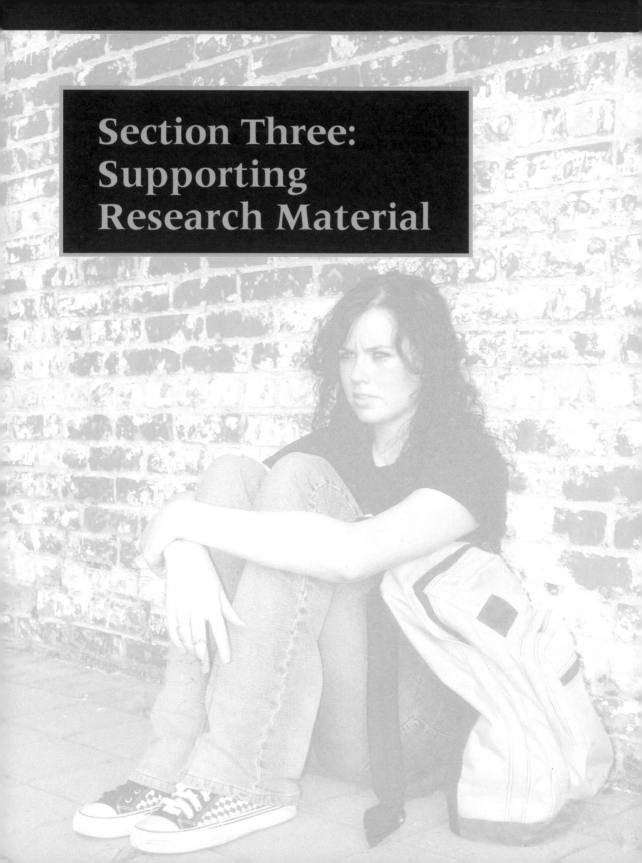

Section Three:
Supporting
Research Material

Facts About Teen Pregnancy

Editor's Note: These facts can be used in reports to rein-force or add credibility when making important points or claims.

Teen Pregnancy in the United States

According to the National Center for Health Statistics:

- Teen birth rates declined steadily from 1991 to 2005—from 60 out of 1,000 girls aged fifteen to nineteen in 1991 to 40.5 out of 1,000 in 2005.
- In 2006—for the first time in fourteen years—the teen birth rate increased 3 percent, to 41.9 births per 1,000 girls ages fifteen to nineteen.
- In 2007 the teen birth rate increased again, by 1 percent.
- The increase occurred in twenty-six states.
- The highest teen birth rates are in the South and Southwest.
  - Mississippi has the highest rate of teen births, with 68.4 per 1,000 girls aged fifteen to nineteen.
  - New Mexico has the second highest, with a rate of 64.1 per 1,000.
  - Texas has third highest, with 63.1 per 1,000.
- The lowest teen birth rates are in the Northeast.
  - New Hampshire has the fewest teen births with 18.7 per 1,000 girls aged fifteen to nineteen.
  - Vermont has the second fewest teen births, with 20.8 per 1,000.
  - Massachusetts has the third fewest teen births, with 21.3 per 1,000.

According to the Guttmacher Institute, a leading authority on sexual and reproductive health:

- Eighty-two percent of teen pregnancies are unplanned.

- Teen pregnancies account for about one in five of all unintended pregnancies annually.
- Eleven percent of all U.S. births are to teens.
- Two-thirds of all teen pregnancies occur among eighteen- and nineteen-year-olds.
- Teen pregnancy rates in the United States are twice as high as in England and Wales or Canada, and eight times as high as in the Netherlands or Japan.
- Seven percent of teen mothers receive late or no prenatal care.
- Babies born to teens are more likely to be low-birth-weight babies than are those born to women in their twenties and thirties.
- Teen mothers are now more likely than in the past to complete high school or obtain a GED, but they are still less likely than women who delay childbearing to go on to college.

According to the New Mexico Teen Pregnancy Coalition:
- The United States has the highest rate of teen pregnancy, birth, and abortion in the industrialized world.
- Nearly four out of ten girls will become pregnant at least once before age twenty.
- Nationwide, teen childbearing costs taxpayers over $38 billion per year.
- Teen mothers are more likely to have serious complications during pregnancy and delivery.
- Teen mothers and fathers are less likely to earn a high school diploma.
- Babies born to teen mothers are more likely to have health problems at birth, be physically abused, abandoned, or neglected, do poorly in school, do time in jail, and become teen parents themselves.

Teens and Sex, Birth Control, and Abortion

The Guttmacher Institute has found the following about teenagers' sexual habits:

- Nearly half (46 percent) of all fifteen- to nineteen-year-olds in the United States have had sex at least once.
- By age fifteen, 13 percent of teens have had sex.
- By the time they reach age nineteen, seven in ten teens have had sex.
- Most young people have sex for the first time at about age seventeen but do not marry until their middle or late twenties; this means that young adults are at risk of unwanted pregnancy and sexually transmitted diseases for nearly a decade.
- The majority (59 percent) of teen girls who have had sex had a first sexual partner who was one to three years older than they were; 8 percent had first partners who were six or more years older.
- Three-quarters—75 percent—of teen females report that their first sexual experience was with a steady boyfriend, a fiancé, a husband, or a cohabiting partner.
- Ten percent of young women aged eighteen to twenty-four who had sex before age twenty reported that their first sex was involuntary. The younger they were at first intercourse, the higher the proportion.
- Twelve percent of teen males and 10 percent of teen females have had heterosexual oral sex but not vaginal intercourse.
- Sexually active teens who do not use birth control have a 90 percent chance of getting pregnant within a year.
- Seventy-four percent of females used contraception the first time they had sex.
- Eighty-two percent of males used contraception the first time they had sex.
- Seventy-one percent of males used a condom the first time they had sex.
- Sixty-six percent of females used a condom the first time they had sex.

- Approximately 25 percent of sexually active teens use two methods of birth control during sex.
- Seventy percent of teens would not get contraceptives from a clinic if they needed their parents' permission.

A 2008 study conducted by the Bradley Hasbro Children's Research Center found:
- Two-thirds—or 66 percent—of sexually active teenagers between ages fifteen and twenty-one did not use a condom the last time they had sex.
- More than 25 percent of participants did not use condoms during the previous three months of sexual activity.

Facts About Parental Involvement Laws

According to the Guttmacher Institute:
- As of 2009, thirty-five states require that a minor seeking an abortion involve her parents in the decision, either by notifying them or by getting their permission.
- Six in ten minors who have abortions do so with at least one parent's knowledge, regardless of state laws.
- The great majority of parents support their daughter's decision to have an abortion.
- Twenty-one states and the District of Columbia allow minors access to contraceptive services without a parent's involvement.
- Two states (Texas and Utah) require parental consent for contraceptive services in state-funded family planning programs.
- Ninety percent of publicly funded family planning clinics counsel teens about abstinence and the importance of talking to their parents about sex.
- Sixty percent of teens who use a clinic for sexual health services say their parents know they are there.

- Among those whose parents do not know, 70 percent say they would not use the clinic for prescription contraception if the law required that their parents be notified.
- One in five teens—about 20 percent—whose parents do *not* know they have access to contraception say they would either have unprotected sex or use the withdrawal method if the law required their parents be notified that they had visited a clinic to receive contraception.
- Only 1 percent of all teens who use sexual health services say they would stop having sex if a law required them to involve their parents in their decision to get prescription contraception.

Facts About Birth Control and Pregnancy

According to the Centers for Disease Control and Prevention, the condom is between 85 to 98 percent effective at preventing pregnancy.

According to Planned Parenthood:
- Less than 1 percent of women who take the pill every day get pregnant.
- The pill is 99.9 percent effective in preventing pregnancy.
- Of women who occasionally miss a dose, eight out of one hundred will get pregnant.
- Starting birth control pills within three days of having unprotected sex reduces a woman's chance of getting pregnant by 75 percent.
- Two out of one hundred women become pregnant when birth control pills are used as emergency contraception within three days of having unprotected sex.
- Taking an emergency contraceptive within seventy-two hours of having unprotected sex reduces a woman's chance of getting pregnant by 89 percent.

- If emergency contraception is taken within three days of having unprotected sex, only one out of one hundred women will become pregnant.

American Opinions on Teen Pregnancy

A 2007 Associated Press–Ipsos poll found the following about American opinions about teens, birth control, and teen pregnancy:

- Thirty-seven percent of Americans think birth control should be provided only to teens who have consent from their parents to receive it.
- Thirty percent think birth control should be provided to all teens.
- Thirty percent think no birth control should be provided to teens.
- Forty-nine percent think making birth control available to teenagers would not encourage teens to have sex any earlier than they would have.
- Forty-six percent think making birth control available to teenagers would encourage them to have sex earlier than they normally would.
- Sixty-two percent of Americans think making birth control available to teenagers would reduce the number of teen pregnancies.
- Twenty-two percent think it would have no effect on the number of teen pregnancies.
- Thirteen percent think it would increase the number of teen pregnancies.
- Fifty-one percent of Americans think emphasizing sex education and birth control can reduce teen pregnancy.
- Forty-six percent think emphasizing morality and abstinence can reduce teen pregnancy.

Finding and Using Sources of Information

No matter what type of essay you are writing, it is necessary to find information to support your point of view. You can use sources such as books, magazine articles, newspaper articles, and online articles.

Using Books and Articles

You can find books and articles in a library by using the library's computer or cataloging system. If you are not sure how to use these resources, ask a librarian to help you. You can also use a computer to find many magazine articles and other articles written specifically for the Internet.

You are likely to find a lot more information than you can possibly use in your essay, so your first task is to narrow it down to what is likely to be most usable. Look at book and article titles. Look at book chapter titles, and examine the book's index to see if it contains information on the specific topic you want to write about. (For example, if you want to write about parental notification laws and you find a book about teen pregnancy, check the chapter titles and index to be sure it contains information about such laws before you bother to check out the book.)

For a five-paragraph essay, you do not need a great deal of supporting information, so quickly try to narrow down your materials to a few good books and magazine or Internet articles. You do not need dozens. You might even find that one or two good books or articles contain all the information you need.

You probably do not have time to read an entire book, so find the chapters or sections that relate to your topic, and skim these. When you find useful information, copy it onto a note card or notebook. You should look for supporting facts, statistics, quotations, and examples.

Using the Internet

When you select your supporting information, it is important that you evaluate its source. This is especially important with information you find on the Internet. Because nearly anyone can put information on the Internet, there is as much bad information as good information. Before using Internet information—or any information—try to determine if the source seems to be reliable. Is the author or Internet site sponsored by a legitimate organization? Is it from a government source? Does the author have any special knowledge or training relating to the topic you are looking up? Does the article give any indication of where its information comes from?

Using Your Supporting Information

When you use supporting information from a book, article, interview or other source, there are three important things to remember:

1. *Make it clear whether you are using a direct quotation or a paraphrase.* If you copy information directly from your source, you are quoting it. You must put quotation marks around the information, and tell where the information comes from. If you put the information in your own words, you are paraphrasing it.

   Here is an example of a using a quotation:

   > Teens have been encouraged to get pregnant by the recent glorification of teen birth in both movies and by Hollywood celebrities. As one reporter has observed, "Unplanned pregnancy is now a pop-culture staple. Movies like *Knocked Up* and *Waitress*, and celebrity moms including Nicole Richie and Jessica Alba, are part of a trend that's sweeping teen culture along with it" (Gulli).

Here is an example of a brief paraphrase of the same passage:

> Teens have been encouraged to get pregnant by the recent glorification of unplanned, out-of-wedlock pregnancy both in movies and by Hollywood celebrities. Movies like *Knocked Up* and *Waitress*, which feature unplanned pregnancies with hilarious and endearing consequences, have made out-of-wedlock surprise pregnancies seem managable and funny, something that gives a person character and definition. Adding to the trend are the pregnancies of celebrity moms like Nicole Richie, Jessica Alba, and even sixteen-year-old Jamie Lynn Spears. Such stories have undoubtedly made teenage girls reconsider pregnancy in a cool and even fashionable light.

2. *Use the information fairly.* Be careful to use supporting information in the way the author intended it. For example, it is unfair to quote an author as saying, "Parental notification laws have the safety of the pregnant teen in mind" when he or she intended to say, "Parental notification laws have the safety of the pregnant teen in mind, but end up putting her in even more danger." This is called taking information out of context. This is using supporting evidence unfairly.

3. *Give credit where credit is due.* Giving credit is known as citing. You must use citations when you use someone else's information, but not every piece of supporting information needs a citation.

    • If the supporting information is general knowledge—that is, it can be found in many sources—you do not have to cite your source.
    • If you directly quote a source, you must cite it.
    • If you paraphrase information from a specific source, you must cite it. If you do not use citations where you should, you are *plagiarizing*—or stealing—someone else's work.

Citing Your Sources

There are a number of ways to cite your sources. Your teacher will probably want you to do it in one of three ways:

- Informal: As in the example in number 1 above, tell where you got the information as you present it in the text of your essay.
- Informal list: At the end of your essay, place an unnumbered list of all the sources you used. This tells the reader where, in general, your information came from.
- Formal: Use numbered footnotes or endnotes. Footnotes or endnotes are generally placed at the end of an article or essay, although they may be placed elsewhere depending on your teacher's requirements.

Works Cited

Gulli, Cathy. "Suddenly Teen Pregnancy Is Cool?" *Maclean's* 17 Jan 2008.

Using MLA Style to Create a Works Cited List

You will probably need to create a list of works cited for your paper. These include materials that you quoted from, relied heavily on, or consulted to write your paper. There are several different ways to structure these references. The following examples are based on Modern Language Association (MLA) style, one of the major citation styles used by writers.

Book Entries

For most book entries you will need the author's name, the book's title, where it was published, what company published it, and the year it was published. This information is usually found on the inside of the book. Variations on book entries include the following:

A book by a single author:
> Axworthy, Michael. *A History of Iran: Empire of the Mind.* New York: Basic Books, 2008.

Two or more books by the same author:
> Pollan, Michael. *In Defense of Food: An Eater's Manifesto.* New York: Penguin, 2009.
> ——. *The Omnivore's Dilemma.* New York: Penguin, 2006.

A book by two or more authors:
> Ronald, Pamela C., and R.W. Adamchak. *Tomorrow's Table: Organic Farming, Genetics, and the Future of Food.* New York: Oxford University Press, 2008.

A book with an editor:
> Friedman, Lauri S., ed. *Introducing Issues with Opposing Viewpoints: War.* Detroit: Greenhaven, 2009.

Periodical and Newspaper Entries

Entries for sources found in periodicals and newspapers are cited a bit differently than books. For one, these sources usually have a title and a publication name. They also may have specific dates and page numbers. Unlike book entries, you do not need to list where newspapers or periodicals are published or what company publishes them.

An article from a periodical:
> Hannum, William H., Gerald E. Marsh, and George S. Stanford. "Smarter Use of Nuclear Waste," *Scientific American* Dec. 2005: 84–91.

An unsigned article from a periodical:
> "Chinese Disease? The Rapid Spread of Syphilis in China." *Global Agenda* 14 Jan. 2007.

An article from a newspaper:
> Weiss, Rick. "Can Food from Cloned Animals Be Called Organic?" *Washington Post* 29 Jan. 2008: A06.

Internet Sources

To document a source you found online, try to provide as much information on it as possible, including the author's name, the title of the document, date of publication or of last revision, the URL, and your date of access.

A Web source:
> De Seno. Tommy. "*Roe vs. Wade* and the Rights of the Father." *The Fox Forum.com* 22 Jan. 2009 < http://foxforum.blogs.foxnews.com/2009/01/22/deseno_roe_wade/ >.

Your teacher will tell you exactly how information should be cited in your essay. Generally, the very least information needed is the original author's name and the name of the article or other publication.

Be sure you know exactly what information your teacher requires before you start looking for your supporting information so that you know what information to include with your notes.

Sample Essay Topics

Teen Pregnancy Is On the Rise

Teen Pregnancy Rates Are Not Increasing

Poverty Causes Teen Pregnancy

Reduced Social Values Cause Teen Pregnancy

Poor Parenting Results in Teen Pregnancy

Availability of Contraception Causes Teen Pregnancy

Availability of Contraception Prevents Teen Pregnancy

Abstinence-Only Education Can Prevent Teen
    Pregnancy

Abstinence-Only Education Encourages Teen
    Pregnancy

Comprehensive Sex Education Can Prevent Teen
    Pregnancy

Comprehensive Sex Education Encourages Teen
    Pregnancy

Teens Should Need Their Parents' Permission to Get an
    Abortion

Requiring Teens to Get Parental Permission for
    Abortion Endangers Them

Teens Should Need Their Parents' Permission to Get
    Emergency Contraception

Teens Are Unlikely to Use Emergency Contraception If
    Their Parents' Permission Is Required

Teens Should Not Be Prescribed Birth Control Without
    Their Parents' Permission

Teens Should Be Prescribed Birth Control Without Their
    Parents' Permission

Parents Have Rights over Their Pregnant Teenagers'
    Bodies

Parents Do Not Have Rights over Their Pregnant
    Teenagers' Bodies

Organizations to Contact

The editor has compiled the following list of organizations concerned with the issues debated in this book. The descriptions are derived from materials provided by the organizations. All have publications or information available for interested readers. The list was compiled on the date of publication of the present volume; the information provided here may change. Be aware that many organizations take several weeks or longer to respond to queries, so allow as much time as possible.

ACLU Reproductive Freedom Project
125 Broad Street, 18th Fl., New York, NY 10004-2400
(212) 549-2500 • Web site: www.aclu.org/reproductiverights

This is a branch of the American Civil Liberties Union that works to guarantee the constitutional right to reproductive choice. The project produces fact sheets, pamphlets, articles, and reports and publishes the quarterly newsletter *Reproductive Rights Update*.

Advocates for Youth
2000 M St. NW, Ste. 250, Washington, DC 20036
(202) 419-3420 • e-mail: info@advocatesforyouth.org
Web site: www.advocatesforyouth.org

Advocates for Youth is the only national organization focusing solely on pregnancy and HIV prevention among young people. It provides information, education, and advocacy to youth-serving agencies and professionals, policy makers, and the media. Among the organization's numerous publications are the brochures *Advice from Teens on Buying Condoms* and *Spread the Word—Not the Virus*. The organization has also launched numerous contraception campaigns to get the word out to teens about the importance of using condoms and the benefits of making emergency contraception available over the counter.

Alan Guttmacher Institute

125 Maiden Ln., New York, NY 10038 • (212) 248-1111
e-mail: info@agi-usa.org • Web site: www.agi-usa.org

The institute works to protect and expand the reproductive choices of all women and men. It strives to ensure that people have access to the information and services they need to exercise their rights and responsibilities concerning sexual activity, reproduction, and family planning. Among the institute's publications are the books *Emergency Contraception Has Tremendous Potential in the Fight to Reduce Unintended Pregnancy* and *Striking a Balance Between a Provider's Right to Refuse and a Patient's Right to Receive Care.*

Catholics for a Free Choice (CFFC)

1436 U St. NW, Ste. 301, Washington, DC 20009
(202) 986-6093 • e-mail: cffc@catholicsforchoice.org
Web site: www.cath4choice.org

This organization promotes family planning to reduce the need for abortion and to increase women's choice in childbearing and child rearing. It publishes the bimonthly newsletter *Conscience*.

Child Trends, Inc. (CT)

4301 Connecticut Ave. NW, Ste. 350, Washington, DC 20008 • (202) 572-6000 • Web site: www.childtrends.org

CT works to analyze contraceptive use among teens and uses statistics and research to educate the teenage population to become consistent users of contraception. The organization produces many publications, including "Facts at a Glance," that incorporates city, state, and national statistics on teen pregnancy, childbearing, and sexuality.

Coalition for Positive Sexuality (CPS)

PO Box 77212, Washington, DC 20013 • (773) 604-1654
Web site: www.positive.org

The Coalition for Positive Sexuality is a grassroots direct-action group formed in 1992 by high school students and activists. CPS works to counteract the institutionalized misogyny, heterosexism, homophobia, racism, and ageism that students experience every day at school. It is dedicated to offering teens sexuality and safe sex education that is pro-woman, pro-lesbian/gay/bisexual, pro-safe sex, and pro-choice. Its motto is, "Have fun and be safe." CPS publishes the pamphlet *Just Say Yes*.

Family Research Council (FRC)

801 G St. NW, Washington, DC 20001 • (202) 393-2100
e-mail: corrdept@frc.org • Web site: www.frc.org

The council is a research, resource, and education organization that promotes the traditional family. It opposes condom distribution programs in schools, and among the council's numerous publications are the papers "Revolt of the Virgins," "Abstinence: The New Sexual Revolution," and "Abstinence Programs Show Promise in Reducing Sexual Activity and Pregnancy Among Teens."

Focus on the Family

Colorado Springs, CO 80995 • (719) 531-5181
Web site: www.fotf.org

Focus on the Family is an organization that promotes Christian values and strong family ties. It campaigns for abstinence until marriage and is opposed to any form of birth control that interferes with fertilization, such as the intrauterine device, or IUD. It has no official position on birth control pills, but it is opposed to emergency contraceptives. It publishes the monthly magazine *Focus on the Family* and sells many books on its Web site that promote abstinence, such as *Wait for Me: Rediscovering the Purity of Joy in Romance*.

Healthy Teen Network

1501 St. Paul St., Ste. 124, Baltimore, MD 21202
(410) 685-0481 • Web site: www.healthyteennetwork.org

Healthy Teen Network is a national organization that focuses on adolescent health issues and is committed to preventing teen pregnancy. It is a network of health specialists, therapists, and reproductive health care professionals that support sexual health for teens at the city, state, and federal level. It puts out many publications, including *Helping Teens Stay Healthy and Safe: Birth Control and Confidential Services* and *A Tool to Assess the Characteristics of Effective Sex and STD/HIV Education Programs.*

The Heritage Foundation

214 Massachusetts Ave. NE, Washington, DC 20002
(202) 546-4400 • e-mail: info@heritage.org
Website: www.heritage.org

The Heritage Foundation is a public policy research institute that supports the ideas of limited government and the free-market system. It promotes the view that the welfare system has contributed to the problems of illegitimacy and teenage pregnancy. Some of the foundation's numerous publications include "Abstinence Education: Assessing the Evidence," "Adolescent Virginity Pledges, Condom Use, and Sexually Transmitted Diseases Among Young Adults," and "Adolescent Virginity Pledges and Risky Sexual Behaviors."

National Abortion and Reproductive Rights Action League (NARAL)

1156 Fifteenth St. NW, Ste. 700, Washington, DC 20005
(202) 973-3000 • e-mail: comments@naral.org
Web site: www.prochoiceamerica.org

NARAL is the nation's leading advocate for privacy and a woman's right to affordable birth control. NARAL works to protect the pro-choice values of freedom and privacy while reducing the need for abortions. It publishes numerous articles, pamphlets, reports, and news briefs about the state of women's access to birth control in America.

National Campaign to Prevent Teen Pregnancy
1176 Massachusetts Ave. NW, Washington, DC 20036
(202) 478-8500 • Web site: www.teenpregnancy.org

The mission of the National Campaign is to reduce teenage and unplanned pregnancy by promoting a combination of abstinence and contraception education for adolescents. The campaign publishes pamphlets, brochures, and opinion polls that include *Not Yet: Programs to Delay First Sex Among Teens*, *The Next Best Thing: Helping Sexually Active Teens Avoid Pregnancy*, and *What Helps in Providing Contraceptive Services to Teens?*

Planned Parenthood Federation of America (PPFA)
434 W. Thirty-third St., New York, NY 10011 • (212) 541-7800
e-mail: communications@ppfa.org • Web site: www
.plannedparenthood.org

Planned Parenthood believes individuals have the right to control their own fertility without governmental interference. It promotes comprehensive sex education and provides contraceptive counseling and services through clinics across the United States. Its publications include the brochures *Guide to Birth Control: Seven Accepted Methods of Contraception, Teen Sex? It's Okay to Say No Way*, and the bimonthly newsletter *LinkLine*.

Project Reality
170 E. Lake Ave., Ste. 371, Glenview, IL 60025
(847) 729-3298 • e-mail: preality@pair.com
Web site: www.projectreality.org

Project Reality promotes an abstinence education curriculum for junior and senior high students. The program is designed to present the benefits of abstinence by using a combination of educational materials and presentations. Research, facts, and statistics are incorporated into the curriculum to demonstrate the dangers of having sex before marriage. The organization works to make teenagers feel pride in their choice to remain abstinent and equips them with the skills to say "no" to sex.

Religious Coalition for Reproductive Choice

1025 Vermont Ave. NW, Ste. 1130, Washington, DC 20005
(202) 628-7700 • e-mail: info@rcrc.org
Web site: www.rcrc.org

The coalition works to inform the media and the public that many mainstream religions support reproductive options, including birth control. It works to make birth control affordable to America's poorest citizens and supports the Prevention Through Affordable Access Act as well as the Responsible Education About Life Act. The coalition also publishes "The Role of Religious Congregations in Fostering Adolescent Sexual Health."

Sexuality Information and Education Council of the United States (SIECUS)

90 John St., Ste. 704, New York, NY 10038 • (212) 819-9770
e-mail: pmalone@siecus.org • Web site: www.siecus.org

SIECUS is an organization of educators, physicians, social workers, and others who support the individual's right to acquire knowledge of sexuality and who encourage responsible sexual behavior. The council promotes comprehensive sex education for all children that includes AIDS education, teaching about homosexuality, and instruction about contraceptives and sexually transmitted diseases. Its publications include fact sheets, annotated bibliographies by topic, the booklet *Talk About Sex*, and the monthly *SIECUS Report*.

Teen-Aid

723 E. Jackson Ave., Spokane, WA 99207 • (509) 482-2868
e-mail: teenaid@teen-aid.org • Web site: www.teen-aid.org

Teen-Aid is an international organization that promotes traditional family values and sexual morality. It promotes abstinence as "saying 'yes' to the rest of your life," and publishes a public school sex education curriculum, *Sexuality, Commitment and Family*, stressing abstinence before marriage. It also publishes several articles, including, "Abstinence Education: Setting the Record Straight," and "An Abstinence Program's Impact on Cognitive Mediators and Sexual Initiation."

Teen STAR Programs

Natural Family Planning Center of Washington, D.C.
8514 Bradmoor Dr., Bethesda, MD 20817 • (301) 897-9323
e-mail: hannaklaus@earthlink.net • Web site: www.teen star-international.org

Teen STAR (Sexuality Teaching in the context of Adult Responsibility) is an international program geared for early, middle, and late adolescence. Classes are designed to foster understanding of the body and its fertility pattern and to explore the emotional, cognitive, social, and spiritual aspects of human sexuality. Teen STAR believes that preaching abstinence and promoting condoms are ineffective ways to educate teens to act sexually responsibly. It publishes a bimonthly newsletter and the paper "Sexual Behavior of Youth: How to Influence It."

Bibliography

Books

Ehrlich, J. Shoshanna, *Who Decides? The Abortion Rights of Teens*. Santa Barbara, CA: Praeger, 2006.

Hall, Meredith, *Without a Map: A Memoir*. Boston: Beacon, 2007.

Jacobs, Thomas A., *Teens Take It to Court: Young People Who Challenged the Law—and Changed Your Life*. Minneapolis: Free Spirit, 2006.

Mathie, Peyton, *Incubator Views: A Story of Teen Pregnancy and the Struggle of Her Preemie*. Bloomington, IN: iUniverse, 2005.

Rose, Melody, *Safe, Legal, and Unavailable? Abortion Politics in the United States*. Washington, DC: CQ, 2006.

Silverstein, Helena, *Girls on the Stand: How Courts Fail Pregnant Minors*. New York: New York University Press, 2009.

Periodicals

Adams, Carla, "SPEAKOUT: Abstinence Education Has Been Effective, *Rocky Mountain News*, March 19, 2008. www.rockymountainnews.com/news/2008/mar/19/speakout-abstinence-education-has-been-effective.

Adams, Jill U., "Teens and the Morning After Pill," *Los Angeles Times*, April 6, 2009.

Amiel, Barbara, "What Mrs. Palin Could Learn from Mrs. T," *Wall Street Journal*, September 5, 2008.

Bixby Center for Global Reproductive Health, "Should Teens Be Denied Equal Access to Emergency Contraception?" 2008. http://bixbycenter.ucsf.edu/publications/files/TeensDenied_2008.pdf.

Blow, Charles, "Let's Talk About Sex," *New York Times*, September 6, 2008.

California Adolescent Health Collaborative, "Involving Parents in Reproductive Health Decisions." www .reproductivejustice.org/download/Prop85/involving_ parents.pdf.

Crosby, Ellen, "The Support the Palins Really Need," *Washington Post*, September 5, 2008.

Crouse, Janice Shaw, "Teen Pregnancy Fact Check," *Washington Times*, September 7, 2008.

Curtis, Barbara, "Sarah Palin *Can* Have It All," *Christian Science Monitor*, September 5, 2008.

Feijoo, Ammie N., "Emergency Contraception: A Safe & Effective Contraceptive Option for Teens," Advocates for Youth, 2005. http://advfy.nonprofitsoapbox.com/ storage/advfy/documents/fsecp.pdf.

Galanos, Mike, "Plan B Risky for 17-Year-Old Girls," CNN. com, May 1, 2009. www.cnn.com/2009/HEALTH/ 04/30/galanos.plan.b/index.html.

Gerson, Michael, "Trig's Breakthrough," *Washington Post*, September 10, 2008.

Katz, Sue, "Maybe We Should Outsource Our Sex Education to Mexico," Alternet.org, June 4, 2008. www .alternet.org/sex/87052.

Keckner, Charles, Testimony before the U.S. House of Representatives Committee on Oversight and Government Reform, April 23, 2008. www.hhs.gov/asl/ testify/2008/04/t20080423a.html.

Kelley-Stamerra, Susan, "Children Deserve a Sex Education Policy That Provides Answers," *Huffington Post,* September 22, 2008. www.huffingtonpost.com/susan- kelleystamerra/children-deserve-a-sex-ed_b_128415 .html.

Los Angeles Times, "Should Doctors Have to Notify Parents Before a Minor Receives an Abortion?" October 22, 2008. www.latimes.com/news/opinion/la-oew- gerace-short22-2008oct22,0,7048163.story.

Lehren, Andrew, and John Leland, "Scant Drop Seen in Abortion Rate If Parents Are Told," *New York Times*, March 6, 2006.

Lithwick, Dahlia, "Bristol's Choice: Republicans and the Illusion of Reproductive Choice," *Slate*. September 5, 2008. www.slate.com/id/2199469.

McGreal, Chris, "Teen Pregnancy and Disease Rates Rose Sharply During Bush Years, Agency Finds," *Guardian* (Manchester, UK), July 20, 2009.

Moore, Kristin Anderson, "Teen Births: Examining the Recent Increase," Child Trends, Research Brief no. 2009-08, March 2009. www.childtrends.org/Files/Child_Trends_2009_03_13_FS_TeenBirthRate.pdf.

MSNBC, "Maine Middle School to Offer Birth Control," October 18, 2007. www.msnbc.msn.com/id/21358971.

NARAL Pro-Choice America, "Emergency Contraception Can Help Reduce the Teen Pregnancy Rate," 2007. www.prochoiceamerica.org/assets/files/Birth-Control-EC-teens.pdf.

Ruse, Cathy, and Austin Ruse, "The Myth of the Contraceptive Compromise," *First Things*, April 1, 2009.

Saletan, William, "Bristol's Body, Sarah's Choice: Abortion, Teen Motherhood, and Parental Authority," *Slate*, September 5, 2008. www.slate.com/id/2199258/pagenum/all/#p2.

Slack, Megan, "Bristol Palin, Candies Foundation Team Up to Fight Teen Pregnancy," *Huffington Post*, May 5, 2009. www.huffingtonpost.com/2009/05/05/bristol palin-candies-fou_n_196838.html.

Stein, Rob, "Teen Birth Rate Rises in U.S., Reversing a 14-Year Decline," *Washington Post*, December 5, 2007.

Weisberg, Jacob, "What Happened to Family Values?" *Newsweek*, September 6, 2008.

Zerbisias, Antonia, "No Movie Endings for Pregnant Teenagers," *Star* (Toronto), January 17, 2008.

Zimmerman, Jonathan, "Poverty, Not Sex Ed, Key Factor in Teen Pregnancy," *San Francisco Chronicle*, September 4, 2008. www.sfgate.com/cgi-bin/article.cgi?f = / c/a/2008/09/04/EDFG12NIUM.DTL#ixzz0Oq6tuLH5.

Web Sites

Abstinence Clearinghouse (www.abstinence.net). This site offers resources on abstinence programs and education. It provides hundreds of resources for teens seeking to remain abstinent until marriage. It also contains a blog where authors discuss the impact of society on teens and sexuality.

Advocates for Youth (www.advocatesforyouth.org). Advocates for Youth promotes the idea that teenagers have a right to sexual and reproductive education. Their comprehensive Web site covers such topics as abstinence, contraception, and HIV/AIDS and STD prevention. AFY believes an informed teenager makes better choices, and the site reflects its dedication to providing adolescents with up-to-date information on sexual health.

Contraceptive Information Resource (www.contracept .org). CIR exists to provide the most up-to-date information on contraception for both men and women. The Web site is designed to educate its readers about the efficacy and failures of various birth control methods as well as assist people with their family planning goals. CIR also provides facts, statistics, and research to help its readers make informed decisions about their sexual health.

Stay Teen (www.stayteen.org). This site, published by the National Campaign to Prevent Teen and Unplanned Pregnancy, has content generated by teens, for teens. Users can upload sex-ed horror stories and watch or produce video ads related to teen pregnancy, sex, contraception, and more.

Teens for Life.com (www.teensforlife.com). This pro-life social networking site and related newsletter seek to educate teens on the issues of abortion, teen pregnancy, and birth control.

Teens Health (http://kidshealth.org/teen/sexual_health/ contraception/contraception.html). This site, maintained by the Nemours Foundation, discusses the choices teens face when confronted with the decision to have sex. Topics covered include general information about birth control as well as on specific methods of contraception, such as the pill, the patch, the ring, injections, and condoms.

Index

should not be needed for abortion, 47–56

Parental involvement laws, 42–45, 49–56

Parents, support for abstinence education by, 22–24

Pharmacists, emergency contraception and, 35–36

Plan B. See Emergency contraception (EC)

Planned Parenthood, 13, 15, 17

Planned Parenthood of Central Missouri v. Danforth (1976), 43

Planned Parenthood v. Casey (1992), 44–45

Q

Quayle, Rich, 35

R

Richards, Cecile, 12–18

Roe v. Wade (1973), 7

Runaways, 54–55, *55*

S

Sex education
abstinence-only, 15–17, 19–24
comprehensive, 12–18, 23–24

Sexual activity, among teens, 13, 21–22

Sexual predators, 36

Sexually transmitted infections (STIs), 14, 22, 34, 37–38

Short, Katie, 45

Suicide, 42

T

Teen birthrates, 16, 21, 48

Teen pregnancy
abstinence-only education reduces, 19–24
adoption and, 7–10
consequences of, 7
emergency contraception can prevent, 25–32
problem of, 13–15
rates of, 48
teaching about birth control reduces, 12–18

Teens
psychosocial development of, 41
risks to, of pregnancy, 13–15
sexual activity among, 13, 21–22
should need parental permission for abortion, 40–46

should not have
  access to emergency
  contraception,
  33–39
should not need parental
  permission for abortion,
  47–56
Teens for Life, 33–39
Texas, 51, 55

U
United Kingdom,
  emergency contraception
  use in, 37–38

W
Waller, Lisa, 25–32
Welfare reform, 21

Picture Credits

About the Editor

Lauri S. Friedman earned her bachelor's degree in religion and political science from Vassar College in Poughkeepsie, New York. Her studies there focused on political Islam. Friedman has worked as a nonfiction writer, a newspaper journalist, and an editor for more than ten years. She has extensive experience in both academic and professional settings.

Friedman is the founder of LSF Editorial, a writing and editing business in San Diego. She has edited and authored numerous publications for Greenhaven Press on controversial social issues such as Islam, genetically modified food, women's rights, school shootings, gay marriage, and Iraq. Every book in the *Writing the Critical Essay* series has been under her direction or editorship, and she has personally written more than twenty titles in the series. She was instrumental in the creation of the series, and played a critical role in its conception and development.